THE TOPICS COVERED IN *THE SECOND HOME BOOK*, FROM A TO Z, INCLUDE:

Appliances, artwork, accoutrements, air-conditioning, alarm systems, alcohol;

Bathrooms, bedding, badly behaved guests, bookshelves;

Cats, construction, cloth napkins, curtains, cooking versus cuisine, Crock-Pots, compost, chores, condo communities;

Discount shopping, dining room tables, DVDs;

Electricians, equipment for sports, emergency plans and supplies, event planning;

Frittatas, furniture painting, footstools, flooring, fire hazards;

Guests, gardeners, glass tub enclosures, glass shelving, getting guests to leave;

Household help, hostess gifts (scary), headboards, hair stylists, home offices, house watchers;

Insects, ice-cream sandwiches, Internet outlets, illnesses, insurance;

Jealousy, job lots;

Kitchens (cabinets, counters, and keeping guests out of), keeping cash on hand;

Lolling, life jackets, larder, laundry rooms, lending (not lending) second homes, laundry baskets;

Mudrooms, mold, making furniture fit, municipal agencies, marital status, medical help;

Nature, neighbors;

Organization, old movies;

Prioritization, painting, plumbing, pots and pans, pools, paying bills, prescription drugs, pests (people and other people's pets), planned communities;

Questions about buying a second home, quagmires of construction;

Reading material, repairing gourmet machinery, rentals (making them yours);

Stepchildren, giving stepchildren space, schlepping, septic tanks, shopping your closet, spaniels, storage, sex, snow;

Table lamps, town dumps, teenagers, to and fro, tax rates, trades people, tennis casseroles;

Upgrading electrical, utilities, using local talent;

Vaccines, vacations (how to actually take one), vegetable gardens, Versailles;

Wicker, window panels, whipped cream, welcoming letter, water, weddings;

Xeroxing everything;

Yearnings;

Zester (citrus), zest for life.

THE

SECOND HOME

BOOK

ALSO BY MARYLOUISE OATES

Making Peace

Writing with Barbara Mikulski

Capitol Offense

Capitol Venture

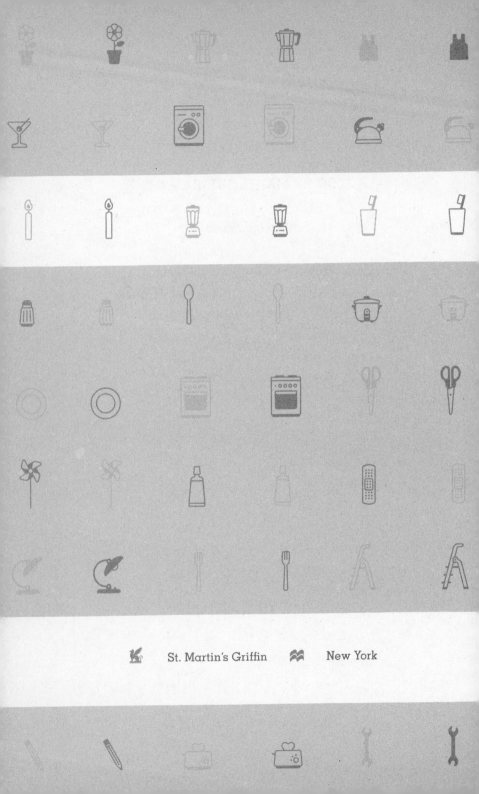

St. Martin's Griffin   New York

THE

SECOND HOME

BOOK

The Can-Do,
How-To,
Get-Through Guide

Marylouise Oates

THE SECOND HOME BOOK. Copyright © 2008 by Marylouise Oates. All rights reserved. Printed in the United States of America. No part of this book may be used or reproduced in any manner whatsoever without written permission except in the case of brief quotations embodied in critical articles or reviews. For information, address St. Martin's Press, 175 Fifth Avenue, New York, N.Y. 10010.

www.stmartins.com

Design by Susan Walsh

Library of Congress Cataloging-in-Publication Data

Oates, Marylouise.
    The second home book : the can-do, how-to, get-through guide / Marylouise Oates—1st ed.
        p. cm.
    ISBN-13: 978-0-312-37474-7
    ISBN-10: 0-312-37474-7
    1. Vacation homes—United States. 2. Second homes—United States.
3. Interior decoration—United States. I. Title.

HD7289.3.U6 O18 2008
643'.250973—dc22

2007047658

First Edition: March 2008

10 9 8 7 6 5 4 3 2 1

To Shrummie

Contents

Acknowledgments

My deep thanks to Dr. Bettyann Ottinger, a psychoanalyst and my dear friend. She conceived this book, telling me it would convince people that having a second home shouldn't make them crazy.

Introduction

For almost twenty years, through no fault of my own, I have frequently owned a second home.

A commuting marriage, a false belief that it would be enjoyable to have a vacation home in the same small town where I spent childhood summers, the moves that accompany happy changes in marital status and career—all these factors stoked my unbridled desire to construct, decorate, entertain, renovate, and generally get my personal life as complicated as possible.

I am not an organizational genius. I am a messy person with a messy life—living in several places with thousands of books, hundreds of piles of papers, dozens of friends who want to brave it all to visit. Out of a deep fear that things are going to tumble down like a beach shack, I have developed plans to bring some order out of chaos. Or at least enough order so that the world thinks I am on top of things—and, sometimes, I am.

My biggest organizing breakthrough was facing the reality of owning a second home. Think of one of those dream sequences in

Spellbound or *Lady in the Dark,* when the heroine cries out some variation of "I know I didn't do it!"

Now I credit my entire life approach to classic black-and-white films, which my mother allowed me to consume like jelly beans. I was raised in a cult, worshipping and watching those movies with Barbara Stanwyck or Norma Shearer or Bette Davis or Kate Hepburn, all with their spotlessly white, creased trousers, running off to play tennis or horseback ride or ski or sail. They were at their second homes—country, alpine, or seashore—and everything was perfect. I foolishly believed that a second house would naturally equate with perfect; weather, guests, food, activities all would blend into a frothy vacation confection. I believed that for about the first week I owned a second home.

Then reality flattened my froth. There would be no creasing of trousers in my second home. I might own an iron, but I didn't have to know its exact location. What needed to be ironed out were some plans, some basic steps for realistically, *not reel*-istically, operating a home that is welcoming to family, guests, and happy times.

At the beginning, there are some basic issues any successful second home owner has to deal with. First, come to grips by answering the haunting question: Why did I get myself into this?

You can choose from the following:

- You thought you were buying a second home to make it easy on yourself—*lolling* is the operative word—around the pool, the field, the beach, the ski lift.
- You thought, as increasing numbers of Americans do, of graciously splitting your life between homes, having

family gamboling around you, vacationing in the healthy outdoors, then packing up and heading back to urban life.

■ You thought old friends would visit, and you would spend happy hours cooking together and playing tennis and swimming and taking long walks. And still more lolling.

■ You thought you could gradually move from your primary home to your second home, which will still feature lots of family and friends and guests and yet more lolling. Perhaps this would accompany a change in career or in career emphasis or would involve, using that red-flag word, retirement.

And your answer: How about all and yet none of the above?

You find yourself scrambling, shopping, schlepping, stewing. Lolling becomes number 22 on your list. And why not?

In your second home, you face all the day-to-day work and aggravations of regular living—with several big "buts." *But* you are not in your most familiar surroundings. *But* you have none of the built-up-over-the-years safety net and support of neighbors and trades people, doctors and handymen, babysitters and dog walkers, not to mention plumbers. *But* you can't figure out what to do first.

You need help. (What you really need is the hot-and-cold running staff from those old movies—"Let me unpack your bag, dear, and whip you up a soufflé"—but that's not in your reach.) What is acquirable is a set of lowered expectations for *luxe* and gracious, along with a higher value for the time you are going to "vacation" at your second home. And you should start right now!

No matter the state of your second home, if there are walls, beds, a bathroom, and something that passes for a kitchen, get in there and commence living. Many questions about fixing, using, improving will only be clear (along with the answers) once you are enjoying the house. A lot of the minor crankiness that can unsettle a second home remains hidden (mice in the basement, bats in the attic, greenhead flies, raccoons that use your trash cans as a gnosh-a-rama, woodchucks under the porch) until someone stirs it up.

Whether you are standing in the middle of a wonderful house that simply needs a little tarting up, or in a wreck that's direct from Rambo the Decorator, it's yours and it should be fun. It's your stage—and whether you want the play to be a soliloquy or involve a cast of thousands, all that matters is your being theatrical and rehearsed enough to pull it off.

There is as much style as substance in having a perfect second home. Make things glamorous: always have fresh tomatoes for your omelets; keep big jars of smelly hand cream beside the guest bed; have a tower of fresh white T-shirts to wear around the house; always cook wearing one good piece of jewelry; and answer every whiny request with "It's my pleasure!" Keep a pile of unread or at least fairly new magazines on the coffee table; have enough gourmet-style olives, snacks, crisps, and cheese on hand to whip up an antipasto at the drop-in of a neighbor—and her guests! Have ten recipes that require little or no preparation and yet taste yummy.

Give it a break. Go easy on yourself—but toughen up your approach. Arm yourself with a forced system of prioritization and organization. If you already own a second home, you can catch up fast. If this is a new venture, get your head around the idea that the more information you accumulate, the less aggravation you will suffer.

You can do all of this, and much more, but only if you get yourself organized.

Who are the already organized anyway?

Some people are very organized because they are very rich, and others—"helpers"—make sure that fresh fruit and flowers and the clean laundry are there to greet the second home owners when they arrive at their cottage/cabin/condo/château/cave/castle.

Some people are organized because they are obsessive, because they keep track of how many stamps they left in each house and when the bills are due and they never, never have to pay a bill on the phone with their credit card.

Some lucky few are minimalists, so they have just what they need and nothing more and their sheets always look ironed and it's all in earth-tones.

Some organized folks are merely cautious souls who never invite the thirteenth person to dinner, never ask the couple barely known to spend a week vacationing with them, and never use the butter left out from breakfast in the luncheon frittata.

All of the above-designated people should not read this book. They don't need it. By means of money, personality, or mania, they have organized lives.

This book gives the rest of us a plan to help organize ours.

One last caveat: Please don't hold yourself to the same standard for "finish," for "spiffy," for "done" that you apply to your primary house. You've fussed over that home for many years, adding ingredients carefully, *à la* a lovely French soufflé. Now you are going to whip up your second home (think Kraft macaroni and cheese), managing to spice it up with a few tasty bits.

Doesn't that sound yummy!

1

Getting Going

It's in the Bag

From day one, you need a second home bag. It can be one of those cute boating bags from L. L. Bean; it can be a leftover diaper bag, or a formerly fashionable tote. It should be roomy but certainly not bigger than a bread box. It cannot be paper. It has to have a sense and spirit of permanence, since it is toting around a chunk of your life. In the bag stick a spiral notebook (available in any drugstore) along with several pens, preferably different colors. Also drop in a "measure"—that's a tape, but carpenters always call it a measure, and saying that makes you sound professional.

Now, walk around your second home and write down the measurements of everything in your notebook. Everything—that includes rooms, closets, the space between the sink and the tub where the toilet sits, the length of the tub, the ceiling height in every room (in any house more than twenty years old, there will be differences), the perimeter of every window, the space between the windows and the ceiling, ditto between the windowsill and the floor, the length of the kitchen cabinets, any wall space in the kitchen that doesn't currently have a cabinet. You get the idea.

Measure everything, inside and out. If it is during a growing season, get your graph paper and chart what is growing where. If it is off season, you'll have to wait until the blooming starts, or check with the former owner or the Realtor. Most owners and real estate agents have photographs of the house taken for advertising. Ask them to dig them out to give you some idea of what you've got.

If this is new construction, you can probably trust the floor plans or blueprints. If someone has lived in the space before you, even one tenant, it is likely that they will have made some adjustments, so you will have to make adjustments on the plans. If you have plans or drawings, put them in the bag. Don't be afraid to fold them. They belong to you. Listen to me: *Stick them in the bag.*

Keep measuring—the appliances (36-inch refrigerators are never just 36 inches), the kitchen sink, the length and width of any hallway, the heights and depths of the closets, the space between the windows in each bedroom (so you know how big a bed you can fit), and the space (if any) between the bathroom medicine cabinets and the top of the sink. Even if you are doing a quick clean and moving right in, you will probably need better closet rods and/or a sense of how much storage you actually have for hanging clothes or stacking sheets. The rule is the older the house, the smaller the closets.

Put all these carefully collected measurements in your notebook. (If you want to be extra careful, make a Xerox the next time you pass a machine, and stick the Xerox in your underwear drawer. No one ever loses anything that has been placed in an underwear drawer.) Along with your measurement-filled notebook, stick in your tote any photograph from a decorating magazine, any sample of fabric or paint (you can tape these into your notebook), any estimate for work to be done, any price quoted for new appliances or windows or fabric. Also make sure you write down every phone and cell number from anyone who has anything to do with your new house. Do not trust inputting these numbers into your cell phone or keeping them on your computer or even writing them down in your phone book. You want a single ready reference for your second home.

Take photographs—especially if you have a digital camera, but a throwaway will do if that is what's available. Take pictures from all sides of the house or condo or apartment. Take at least one picture of each room from each corner in the room. In the kitchen, take photos of all the appliances. Photos are key, especially if you are going to be making long-distance decisions. The photos remind you that there are three drawers on the left side of the stove, shelves above the poles in the closets and a vanity under the sink in the guest bathroom. They help in several other ways: they will answer those nagging questions of how many windows really are in the living room; they will help you think about furniture for the house, along with window treatments and lighting; they will assist in making color choices. That last one seems a stretch, but when you are sitting with seventeen various shades of celadon on teeny little pieces of paper, it does help to remind your eye what the room you are going to paint actually looks like.

> "This floor used to be wood but I had it changed. Valentino
> said there's nothing like tile for the tango."
> **Gloria Swanson to William Holden, *Sunset Boulevard* (1950)**

This does not, repeat *does not*, resemble moving into a primary residence. You want to get this place up and running at quickly as possible so you can actually enjoy it. You are going to take some shortcuts. You are also going to be frugal. It doesn't matter that you are well fixed enough to own second home. You be the judge of which shortcuts you will take and what splurges you will indulge.

It's all about control. You get to decide when enough is enough. You are so lucky to have this second home—and now you get to put emotion aside for a few minutes and make some hard-core plans.

A Little Tarting Up

You have bought a second home. You have learned the second home mantra (it practically comes with the mortgage papers): "We are just going to move in and see how it all works. And then, in a couple of years, we'll get rehabbing under way."

I've done that. I've lived with kitchen counters built for people whose previous home was on the Yellow Brick Road; I've cooked at stoves that were probably designed by the man who invented fire; I had one minor project that kept carpenters in my home for so many months that they would make the coffee when they arrived in the morning; I had a painter in Los Angeles many years ago (where those in the contracting business are frequently out-of-work actors) who got a recurring role as a baby-faced killer and could only paint in alternating weeks; I had another painter who had a day job, not as a painter, and loved painting late at night, just about one A.M. (I'll put up with almost anything for a fabulous faux finish.)

On minor repairs or cosmetic work, there is a certain attitude that has to be adopted in dealing with skilled workers—plumbers and electricians being chief among them, painters and carpenters less so. The same deep-breathing exercises used for natural child-birth are helpful, as are any spiritual guides to peace and contentment. What skilled craftsmen usually believe is that you need them more than they need you. And, amazingly, they're right on target. So try to fit your schedule to theirs, and never, on a small but urgent job, feel embarrassed at offering a little extra cash.

I always feed everybody who works fixing up any house I'm working on. Not every day, and certainly not always with home-cooked food. But I try, if there is a weeklong job, to offer to buy the pizza or the subs or the lobster rolls at least once during that week. I make coffee and offer it. And I make sure always to ask everyone on the job their name and I introduce myself. This is especially important in a second home, where you might be coming and going and want to be sure that you have made a good impression on the craftsperson. Besides, it's the polite thing to do.

Eschewing major construction and all it entails, here are some random pointers that may be helpful in doing smaller jobs:

- Painting: For small paint jobs, always check the "returned paint" rack in a Home Depot store. A can of customized paint, ordered by a customer who suffers second thoughts and never takes it out of the store, usually costs around $5.

- Painting: If your second home is in a fancy area, you might be thinking about custom-finish painting, i.e. striating, fauxing, stenciling. Do not rely on a photograph of a job that the painter supposedly did in someone else's house. Get a sample of the custom-finish on a board, with the colors you want to use in your home. Then you will know that this particular painter actually knows how to do that particular technique.

- Painting: All whites are not created the same and nowhere is this more apparent than in a bathroom. Even a teensy difference between wall color and wall tile can be jarring. Check and double check. Buy the tiny bottle that many paint stores will sell you—usually about $5— and put it on the wall next to the tile.

- Painting: The job always takes longer than you expect, and you can't put up drapes/shades/blinds until the painting is done. You are living in the house and would like to walk through the kitchen without being on display for the whole neighborhood. Go to Bed Bath and Beyond, Lowe's or any large hardware store. Buy the nifty little pleated paper shades that stick on to the wood or the glass itself. Cost: about $7 a window, and they are surprisingly sturdy. You are out of the spotlight.

- Wallpapering: My dear, you are ambitious! Good wallpaper comes in lots. So if you need six rolls, make sure the numbers of the rolls are in order, i.e. no. 17 through no. 22. This is especially important if you are shopping for wallpaper at an outlet or clearance sale. Even if the rolls are in the same box, check out the numbers.

■ Electrical: If you are having piecemeal electrical work done, make sure that the electrician has a written list of exactly which switches should operate what lights. If you leave the light-switch decision in the hands of the electrician, you will wind up turning on the living room lights from the upstairs bedroom. We lived for years at the Cape with what I came to think of as random lighting—it was always a guess as to what switch worked which set of cans or plugs.

■ Electrical: If you are installing a dishwasher, a microwave, a garbage disposal, or a monster fridge where none existed before, you must upgrade your electrical. And when you do, ask for designated lines for the devices that really suck up the juice. That is the only way to make sure that you can wash the clothes, the dishes, and warm-up supper simultaneously.

■ Electrical: If you are more into primitive and have purchased or live in a home that still has a fuse box, give it a break. This is not safe. Upgrade at once to circuit breakers.

■ Plumbing: Someday, somehow, you will need a plumber. It's a fact of life. Maybe you see a plumbing truck at a nearby neighbor's and go by to introduce yourself, a potential new customer. Maybe that plumber is retiring, has too much business already, or simply seems like a mean, nasty no-goodnik when you talk to him. Over the years, I have asked plumbers how they would find a plumber. (So you haven't had that kind of conversation, huh? Well, do *you* have a good plumber?) Repeatedly, in small towns, plumbers tell you to check with the Chamber of Commerce. Established businesses join the chamber—businesses that want to connect with the community. Also, it is not such a bad idea, when you think you have located a decent plumber, to set up an appointment and go through the house. Pay the plumber for his time. See if he shows up on time—or at least on the same day. Plumbers are just like lawyers, except lawyers have to deal with a lot of stuff a decent plumber wouldn't touch.

■ For all jobs: Make a list of what you want done. A punch list, as the boys call it. It doesn't matter how minor— hanging up a robe hook on the back of a bathroom door or putting in a new screen—make a list. First, if you don't, you will forget what you asked the worker to finish, especially easy when you are running two houses. Second, you will have no proof of what you asked the worker to do when it turns out he didn't finish the job. A list doesn't solve all problems. No matter how many times you set up an appointment for a skilled worker in a primarily second home community, you have a better-than-even chance that an "emergency" somewhere else will keep your worker in that other place. It seems illogical that a carpenter or painter has an urgent duty: "Quick, give me a faux finish in my powder room or I will simply die!" No, but they have seen electricians and plumbers pull this stunt, and they have listened and learned.

Shopping Your Closet

I am a lifelong admirer of Richard Scarry, his wonderful children's books and their characters, Huckle Cat, Bananas Gorilla, Mr. Frumble, and my favorite, Lowly Worm, as in the classic Scarry sentence: "Lowly was getting dressed. He put on his shoe."

Since I live in more than one place, I often think of Lowly as I deal with the one-shoe-in-this-house dilemma. But that is not my point. Scarry wrote all those wonderful, complexly illustrated and sly books, showing how the everyday things that people do are fascinating and fun when they are done by animal characters. That's how I feel about furnishing a second home. It's playing house. Chores and choices that are routine in putting together your primary residence become captivating and charming when they are part of building your second venue.

To begin: If you are living in the normal, American middle-class home, you have extra stuff. Towels, silverware, kitchen chairs, sheets, mugs with cocker spaniels, or "I Love Toledo" on them. You have the pillows you took off your bed when you bought the new ones that you've now used for three years. (If you are in more luxurious financial circumstances or you have limited closet space, you tossed those old pillows—and as soon as you did, you hated the replacement ones.)

With so much stuff, it might seem as though you can troll your primary house and, except for a sofa and three box springs and mattresses, you will be able to furnish your new second home. Think again. You are not going to all this expense to have a home you envision as restive or exciting or both, and then fill it with secondhand stuff you'd be embarrassed to contribute to a neighborhood garage sale. (The exceptions would be people directly descended from the Mayflower, who seem to be able to make any piece of shredded or peeling furniture look exceedingly chic. We all missed that boat!)

Some of your already-owned stuff will work. Notice my use of language. Most used cars are "used." But luxury cars are always "pre-owned." Think of your good stuff as befitting this description. But be warned: A chair you detest but send to temporarily reside in your second home will put down roots. Your partner or housemate will develop an inordinate fondness for it. The cat will become even more attached to it. This disliked chair will never, never, never go away. So, please, you've seen enough horror movies: Don't ever move anything into your second home that is truly nasty. Better you should invite a goblin home to dinner.

As you shop your primary house, your first job is to classify everything extra into three broad categories:

- Absolutely okay/pre-owned—I wouldn't be embarrassed if my ex-husband, ex-roommate, or ex-employer saw it.
- Might make it, but only until I get something better.
- Now I can finally get rid of it.

This is also a good time to look at what is actually furnishing or accenting your primary residence to see if there is something there you want to upgrade. Send the slightly used stuff to the country or the mountain.

My favorite transferables are drinking glasses, cloth napkins, bed linens, pots and pans, cooking utensils, throw pillows, soap dishes, television sets (no matter what you say, you will *too* watch TV in your vacation home), paperback books, especially the ones from college with the underlining, and cotton bathrobes. You will be tempted to include the vacuum cleaner you bought on a whim at the discount store. Forget it. You don't want it in your primary residence; you won't use it in your second home. Give it away.

The second home will become *your* house much quicker if you bring things that are old favorites and that add a mildly layered look. I was given a lovely velour throw several years ago. Sabrina, my Clumber spaniel, had a hankering one day and ate a big hole through one end of it. No matter. I used it for several years at the Cape house because nobody could see the big hole as long as the throw was draped over the back of a sofa, pretty and still convenient for afternoon naps. A favorite friend had given it to me, and, the few times someone out of the immediate family wrapped themselves up in it, I could tell the highly amusing story of my ill-behaved dog who consumes throws. (Oddly, after that first adventure in velour, Sabrina never went back for a second bite, even though she would frequently lie on the sofa, throw adjacent.)

Speaking of throwing, a second home is a great place to throw around cotton paisleys, usually sold as either tablecloths or bed-spreads. Buy several with colors that match and simply throw them on the mismatched furniture in your living room. They are also great if you have dogs who believe the sofa is their bed, since the paisleys—check this out—are now colorsafe and machine washable.

No matter how sparse or shabby the furnishings you begin with, in a second home you must put some things on the wall. If you are into a buying mode, eBay is a good first stop and cheaper than the neighborhood chi-chi gallery. There are hundreds of "local artists" trying to sell their stuff on eBay and some of it turns out to be quite attractive and usable. Even better, if you have a series of old family photos that are sitting in a drawer, get them out. It's easy to do a quick frame job on a half-dozen photos and instantly have art that goes up the staircase or, better yet, gives people something to look at in the powder room.

Warning: If you are at the beginning of settling your second home, do not get into artsy-craftsy nonsense. No sewing, quilting, refinishing, matting, potting, or working with collages, to say the least. These loving-hands-at-home activities, which consume your time and energy, are practical only if you've practiced them for years—or if you are an elf in the hollow of a tree. Keep the goal in sight and don't be led down a project path littered with half-done seashell-adorned picture frames or end tables with artwork that comes unglued.

Instead, track down those already framed photographs that have wound up in your hall closet. No, no silver allowed. Too fancy and it needs polishing. Metal frames (even bronze for door handles and window locks) are off-limits at the beach or the lake. You just don't know what will pit or turn. It might say on the label that it is "rust resistant," but that is highly unlikely. Framed "art" that has migrated to the attic or the basement could be utilized—you remember those movie posters, antiwar posters, political posters,

museum posters that your primary home has grown too sophisti-
cated or crowded to handle. How about those souvenirs from
trips to Mexico or Canada or Puerto Rico? (With the payments on
your second home, you won't be traveling much, so at least enjoy
the memories.) How about those straw hats or baseball caps or
books about 1960s Southern California architecture that you have
never opened since the day you bought them? Those are all perfect for a second home.

Things that belonged to your family are fabulously nice
touches—a small glass bowl beside your bed to put your rings in
at night, a pretty plate to put on a table beside the door for your
keys. But not your great-aunt's gold-rimmed china, now service
for seven since the dinner party three years ago when some klutz
volunteered to help clear the table. These dishes have to be hand-
washed and you never thought them attractive. Give them or con-
sign them to a thrift shop. Your aunt would appreciate that. She
was always charitable.

Think about your books.

At the beach, nothing is better for you or worse for the books
than salt air. Ditto art work on paper. You don't want to bring
along a favorite print unless you are willing to agree that you want
it in this particular house—and you don't care if it doesn't make it
into the next house or the next century. You can help protect art on
paper by having a piece reframed by a knowledgeable craftsperson, one who will know the kind of backing and protective sealer
best in your part of the earth. But no one can frame a print on paper and guarantee that it is absolutely dampness-proof.

If you are going to work at your second home and your work requires bound volumes, invest in a lawyer's bookcase, the kind with the glass doors. And ask the people at your local closet or container store to recommend the best mold-dampness preventative. Also, go on-line. I can hardly believe the number of people who want to either sell or chat about antidampness products.

Air-conditioning, of course, is the sad but true solution to humidity and the paper purges it inflicts. If you green-up and decide to no longer use air-conditioning, your books and paper will "green-up" with mold. Perhaps a reasonable, environmentally good solution would be to occasionally run the air-conditioning just to get the stickiness out of the house. This is certainly a personal and political decision.

Of course the art that thrives in moisture is an oil painting. Think of Venice, with or without the flooding. My beach house is crammed with seascapes, mostly in oil, one superb, a few from an artist neighbor, a couple from eBay, and some from nearby second-hand shops. Think of them as Young Masters.

2

Furnishings

First—the Big Stuff

It's your house and your taste. I'm covering the bedroom, kitchen, closets, etc., in separate chapters, but here are my basic rules:

- **Make sure what you bring is comfy—and sturdy.** There is a lot more flopping on furniture in a second home. You will be amazed at how people curl themselves up on sofas and chairs—in ways they would never do in a primary residence. Part of it is your fault, because you've made it so cozy. So live with it—up to a point. I object when visitors believe that any piece of furniture in a second home is a footstool in disguise. Even at the dining-room table, they will stretch out their legs and stick their tootsies on a nearby chair. Stop them. That's carrying comfy too far. But do think of yourself as being trapped between a rock and a soft place: A second home is for relaxing and that means, depending on your bent, either stretching out or curling up.

- **Anything can be painted white**. That's exactly what those fancy sloppy-chic stores do. They start with good, strong furniture—not particularly stylish, but real wood. The kind of stuff your grandmother threw out years ago— and now you regret her foolishness. For heavens sake, don't paint anything you think might be antique—drag it or a photo of it to the nearest reputable dealer and ask. Or go online via eBay, and see if anything similar shows up. Once you've protected yourself from sanding away the fortune you would get for a Chippendale chair, do some work with fine sandpaper and paint it. Or the bureau. Or the bedstead. Or even the kitchen table. I am not advocating doing a "finish." If you want to go down that road, you will go it alone. I don't go there. But you can paint furniture white and it perks it up quite well.

- **Rattan and wicker are good—sometimes.** Even the rattiest rattan or wicker can be held together for another season with a big infusion of spray paint. And dressed up with a cheapo pillow from one of the cheapo stores. Furniture can also migrate, as it ages and you get fancier with your style, from indoors to outdoors. My warning is that wicker can be wickedly weak—and all those coats of paint don't make the seat secure. Really check out what is happening under the pillows as the years go by.

- **Big furniture sales mean never having to say full price.** Gone are days of the twice-annual furniture sale.

At most of the national department stores, any minor national holiday is a reason for much ballyhooed sales and significant mark-downs. One advantage of these stores is that you can shop in either of your communities. You can actually choose the furniture you want while in your primary home neighborhood, but then have it delivered from the store's local outlet to your second home. Now, I would never buy a bedroom set or any kind of a dining-room extravaganza from a department store, since it seems they all come with nineteen separate pieces— tables, breakfronts, etc.—so that you would need a Mc-Mansion to house them. But I am nuts for their sofas and their modular sofa units.

■ **Click into chic.** All of the national hip furniture chains — Restoration Hardware, Mitchell Gold, Pottery Barn, Room & Board, and Crate & Barrel—are available on the Web. If you are in a terrible rush, you don't need to know that they have regular sales and several of them even have outlet stores, which you can find on their individual Web sites. All of them, whether you are buying from a local store or via the Web, impose a delivery charge, frequently quite hefty, so be sure to factor that in to the costs.

■ **The kitchen and/or dining room table must hold eight (to ten) people.** Don't panic. That's why the gods created leaves. If your place is small, look for a narrow, Parsons-style table that you can tuck behind the sofa when you are not entertaining. You only need a 26-inch-wide table to accommodate people sitting across from each other and having their dinners on normal plates and enjoying a glass of wine. I had a narrow table for years, and, as they say about socialites, a table just can't be too thin. You insist that you will never have that many people to dinner. Why limit yourself! Also, if you are going to use this house/condo/hut/A-frame on a regular basis, you will probably need some work space—to go onto your computer, to do your taxes, to allow your grandchildren to paint the shells they found on the beach. Trust me. Get the table!

■ **Look for a big, fat coffee table that becomes the center of your life.** The best one I found, and I got it at their outlet, is from Restoration Hardware. It is humongous, with pillars between the actual coffee table and the shelf underneath. On top, I have an old Russian lacquered box for storing cocktail napkins, along with a pewter-edged white ceramic tray from my friend Andrea and some lovely stone coasters from my son Michael. These are treasured things and they make the table work, whether it is simply as a spot to pop down my coffee cup or as a gathering place for predinner drinks. Scads of things to read wind up on the bottom shelf. The table is in front of the fireplace, so it's great to have supper on in the winter.

■ **Anything can be cut to fit.** That includes china closets or breakfronts. Frequently, in a second home, a secondhand breakfront is the way to go, since you get a lot of storage bang for your bucks. Perhaps you find a huge one at a secondhand store, but your ceiling is too low. Easily fixed. Cut the piece in half—there's a good chance it already splits in the middle. Trim the bottom of the upper half, then plop it back on its base. What if you have a table too snug for dining, but still in good shape? Cut down the legs to a 17 to 19-inch height and you have the perfect coffee table. In warmer climes, keep your eyes peeled at end-of-season sales for rattan card tables or game tables, which transform beautifully into coffee tables.

■ **Buying secondhand furniture is fraught with dangers!** Bedbugs are back! Not seen much around campus for many decades, bedbugs returned with a bang during the past ten years. They're back at their old favorite haunts— hiding in small crevices, they stow away in furniture, especially mattresses and beds. Used furniture has the greatest risk of harboring bedbugs and their eggs. But you can also find the teeny devils in wooden chairs and even in old books. They are hardy eaters—they feed on the blood of mammals—but can live months in a vacant apartment waiting for the next arrival of oak and chintz. The Harvard School of Public Health has an excellent Web site that will explain how you get them and how to get rid of them. Their Web site address is: *http://www .hsph.harvard.edu/bedbugs/.*

■ **Make books part of your furniture.** This is accomplished in two ways: one, put small bookcases in any nook or cranny (what *is* a cranny anyway?); or two, steal an idea from my pal Joan, whose second home is in Paris. She uses coffee-table art books that never get opened as, if not coffee tables, end tables! You can stack the books as high as you deem safe and plop down a small lamp, a couple coasters, and you're done.

■ **Bookshelves don't have to be forbidding.** I have perfect bookshelves, and they are only seven inches deep. Wait! Go and get your measure (it is in your second house tote, of course) and see how deep most of your books are. Right! Except for art books, they all fit on a seven-inch-deep shelf. You can easily have your carpenter build a wall of book shelves that are only seven inches deep—and cheap—because you use the existing wall as the backing of the unit and you make the shelves a set height. (If you must have backing, sheets of ready-made bead board are perfect!) These shelves should be attached to the wall for stability. Books are great sound insulators and are good if you are trying to give a bedroom a little more privacy. Also, before the carpenter installs the backless shelves, paint the wall where they are going a bright color that contrasts with or complements the rest of the room. My little office has one bead board wall, original to the house. (Bead board is a grooved plywood, frequently used as wainscoting.) The room is painted white, but the wall behind the bookshelves is painted navy blue. Very snappy!

■ **Beware of over-accessorizing.** You are not going to be there all the time and, though I am not a minimalist, I must remind you to either put away—or prepare to dust—any cute things you have on side tables and end tables. Also, only go down the many-framed-snapshots-on-a-table road knowing there is no escape. You go out and buy several nice frames; friends come, you take pictures and place them in the frames. These frames are there forever, because people want to see themselves when they come back. (I personally love pictures of my friends and especially pictures of my friends' kids and grandkids. But I tend toward the layered!) One solution is a series of large, matted montage photo frames. I have several with pictures of one of my husband Bob's significant birthdays. Almost all our closest friends were here, and now they are immortalized on a staircase wall.

■ **Beware of hostess gifts.** Try to avoid the gifts that keep giving, living a long and unattractive life in your second home. Direct friends, when they are courteous enough to ask, to bring "something we can eat, drink, or enjoy together during the visit." My favorites are wine, coffee, olive oil, movies, CDs. My pal David once sent me a glamorous Italian umbrella stand and has, over the years, built up my DVD selection. I got great notepaper with my Cape house address from Fred and a Brisker for my kitchen from my dear friend Anne. (For the uninitiated, a Brisker is a plug-in bread box that holds off staleness from breads and crackers.) All very usable and attractive. However, whatever a close friend gives you, keep track, so even if you don't use that particular lighthouse-shaped pitcher, you can drag it out when they come again. On the other hand, is there anything nicer than a cotton throw for a beach house? We've received several over the years and they add a bright tone and a homey feeling.

- **Have somewhere to put magazines.** That doesn't seem complicated, until you try to figure it out. You want to leave stacks of them around, because—say with *The New Yorker* or *The Economist*—you really *are* going to get around to reading that twenty thousand-word article on anxiety or on mulching in the Maldives. My solution is an old-fashioned metal newspaper stand that I found in a second-hand store. It sits on the sunporch, stuffed with magazines. Every few weeks, I run a minor purge and make space for new arrivals.

- **Have footstools.** This will let you cut down on the number of chairs, but you still have lots of seating if you are having a party. Also, they double-up as end tables, especially if you plunk a tray, plastic or metal or woven, on top. (And perhaps guests will use them for their feet.)

- **Please make the chairs comfortable for every size and shape.** Sometimes, in a rush for authenticity, there is an embracing of wicker and twig. These ever-popular manifestations of beach and country can be killers, especially if people are in shorts. Nasty! If you are committed to such furniture, put big chair pads on them, and plenty of pillows. You can also err by specializing in huge upholstered chairs that trap the unaware, fabric versions of the man-eating flower in *Little Shop of Horrors*. Make sure you include at least one or two simple wooden armchairs or rockers, either with a chair pad or an upholstered seat. Many, many people have back trouble and are fearful of drowning in the upholstery abundance.

- **Hemp rugs and pets don't mix.** The darlings might think it is real grass and you know what grass means to a pooch. Once that has happened, it is impossible to get stains or smells to disappear completely. And, honestly, don't all those grassy things have kind of a smell, anyway? They might be perfectly fine in a tropical area, but anywhere else—I don't think so.

- **Don't dis the locals.** When you are looking for cabinets, faucets, toilets, chest of drawers—check out the independent stores near your second home. It is not always true that the chain stores offer the best deals. If you are shopping off season, you may strike a deal with the mom-and-pop appliance store or cabinetmaker.

- **Shop the warehouse sales.** Especially if you live near a major metropolis, the fabric and furniture sales held when brand-name manufacturers clean out their overstock are really worthwhile. In New York, you can plan your shopping by signing up for a free, online subscription to www.dailycandy.com. In other major cities, you need to watch the sales column in the monthly city magazines. Also, *HomeDecorators.com* and *BallardDesigns.com* have great Internet sales and are always worth a visit.

Eventually, you will come to the touchy question of hiring a decorator.

Realize that all decorators are not defined equally—some decorate, some shop, some supervise construction; others come in to "install" your house. There are decorators who get hired to find specific pieces of furniture—a dining room table, chairs for a sun porch, an antique coatrack. They get paid by the hour—or they take a markup on what they find for you. Some decorators take that markup on what the piece would cost retail, even though they get it wholesale via their "decorator's number," and charge full retail plus the markup. Other decorators charge you the percentage of the retail as their markup, but add that to the lower wholesale they paid for the piece. Some decorators charge a design fee that you pay up front, and then you pay directly for the furniture, either wholesale or retail—whatever they can work out.

Complex? Yes, so go cautiously into this world, especially if you are doing your second home from far away. You might really need somebody to take charge of the whole operation—so you decide that it is worth the money to pay a professional to make your second house work for you, and work fast. If so, set some ground rules. Are you willing to live with what the decorator can find in the showroom, or do you want things "special," which translates as special orders for fabrics or finishes, which translates as waiting perhaps months for delivery? Do you have colors in mind, or do you want the decorator to come up with a scheme for your approval? Do you have pieces already in your possession that you want your second home "look" built around? Are you big or little people? Do you want puffy furniture or something more Shaker?

And, the most important question: What is your budget?

You must set a limit and you must tell it to your decorator. It is so easy to buy into buying "some darling toile slip-covered chairs" that indeed you yearn for until you see the price tag. Put a lid on it. Tell the decorator that you will go to *this* cost level and no higher. Within that budget, make priorities. Make a list, with the decorator, of the must-haves. Don't budge from it. You know how you are going to use your second home—or at least you have some idea of whether you want a giant television set or a long buffet; do you need kids' rooms or guest rooms or home offices?

Color is a big question. The moment someone babbles on about their "color palette" I want to run for my Crayola box. Among decorators there is some deep-seated impetus to make every house within sight of ocean or bay into a blue-and-white manse. (I adore blue-and-white and it is the color of my tidy wee office. But just because you're seaside, you haven't joined the Greek navy.) You don't have to have pseudo-Indian blankets over the back of chairs that have been fashioned from elk horns, even if your second home is in the Great Northwest. You don't want a baroque brocade if you are bayside, but, on the whole, the style of your house is what you want. Don't let geography dictate a total approach— nor let a decorator dictate what you really want.

If you are worried about becoming a decorator victim, a hostage to someone else's taste and yet insecure about your own, your only solution is to make some primary decisions. Put down some markers. If you can't bring a strong design sense to your first meeting with the decorator, at least bring a piece of fabric that you think would work somehow in the house or some photos from decorating magazines. Hey, who do you think buys these publications, anyway? People—and decorators—who want to have other options and other ideas. Talk through with the decorator what ambience—that's a five-dollar word meaning feeling or mood—should prevail in your second home. Then tell the decorator the colors you favor, what special furniture or art or fabrics you want surrounding you in your second home. Continue, until

Kathleen Brown is a lifelong Californian, now the head of Goldman Sachs Public Finance for the Western United States and the former California treasurer. She and her husband, retired news executive Van Gordon Sauter, commute constantly—with great style.

Every weekend when I drive from L.A. to the desert, I plan a stop at Costco in Palm Desert to buy bunches of fresh flowers—roses, sunflowers, lilacs, tulips, whatever is in stock. They are a bargain so I get double what I could in LA. I arrive and the first thing I do is clip the stems and arrange my bouquets to place around the house. Satisfied that the "sunshine" is spread around the interior of our desert retreat, I relax for the weekend. When Sunday arrives all too quickly, I am unwilling to leave the treasured flowers behind. So, I ritualistically wrap them in wet paper towels, put them plastic grocery bags, place them in a short plastic waste basket, cart them to the car, carefully place them wedged in a safe place and then drive them home to L.A., where I repeat my arrangements in our city apartment. My husband thinks I am crazy, but it has become part of the rhythm of my peripatetic life.

you have made your decisions, to give her or him additional photographs of rooms or furniture or fabrics that catch your fancy.

Decorators are a good if you need them, and if you use them and they don't use you. It's as simple as that.

Let There Be Light

Or at least table lamps.

Don't skimp on lamps. The quickest way to make your cottage or condo resemble a shack is to make it dark. Cozy is the operative word, and warmth comes from light.

Lamp lighting is especially easy when Target, Marshall's, and Home Goods have such attractive, inexpensive, and safe models. It's frequently the last thing on everyone's furnishing list, though it should be on top. If you are planning long evenings in your second home, playing Scrabble or reading, you have to be able to see what the little letters spell out! And you will need, at least in the first months in your new place, to make it as user-friendly as possible. Nothing does that better than lamps.

New lamps, that is. Do not, repeat, *do not* bring those cranky antique lamps from your attic into your second home. Leave them unplugged and in the primary home—unless you have them rewired. Putting a frayed lamp cord into a fraying electrical system—and why haven't you had an electrician upgrade it?—is a short circuit to disaster. Floor lamps are a real necessity in a second home, especially if your living room is going to serve several purposes, i.e. reading, TV watching, game playing, entertaining. You can easily change form and function by pulling a lamp out from behind a chair and setting it next to a card table. You can make a comfy reading area by using a floor lamp between two chairs and a teensy table in front of it.

Not that I neglect table lamps. And nothing perks up those little devils better than a new shade. For me, the best way to get the right shade is to take the lamp with you to the store. Doesn't matter if it's Ye Old Lamplighter's Expensive Boutique or Target—you cannot tell how a shade will look simply by measurements. Lamp in hand, you can see if the shade you like fits well on the "harp"— that's the curvy piece of metal that sticks into those little metal openings on both sides of the light bulb. The harp holds the shade in place. As you try various shades, you need to figure out whether in addition to a new shade you need a smaller or larger harp, readily available in hardware stores or lamp stores. Your shade should cover the mechanics of the lamp without making the lamp look like one of those dancing mushrooms from *Fantasia*. Sadly, if you live near salt water, you will discover that most harps come in brass. They will turn and there is nothing you can do about it.

As long as you are sprucing up your lamps, how about some new finials, the little screw-in gizmos that hold the shade in place at the top of the harp? No, you certainly don't need them—but I have a penchant for fancy finials. They come in an abundance of styles and degrees of kitsch, from pieces of Murano glass to lighthouses or baby Swiss chalets. I find them all very cheery.

As you light up and tart up your second home, you will need to look skyward—at your ceilings. If it is an older home, from the beginning of the last century, it's more than probable that you won't have ceiling lights. Perhaps there are still old sconces on the wall, or cover plates where such lights used to be. Move ahead with caution. Perhaps the electrician is telling you that he can just punch up into that ceiling and put in some cans and it will be hunky-dory. Don't you believe it.

Electricians are the Labrador retrievers of the building trades. They are friendly and so willing to do anything you ask—but, like those Labs, electricians leave a terrific mess wherever they go and they don't seem to understand the consequences of their actions, i.e. punching creates a pile of plaster and paint on the floor, crumpled up chunks of wire and wallboard, dust everywhere.

And yet, you just can't have a home without electricians. You *must* use a licensed electrician—and this is something to check out personally—to upgrade your system, if it needs it. Your insurance carrier will not be happy if your home burns down and it turns out Handy Harry played around in the fuse box. One warning: Any other job you need an electrician for should require you doubling the cost estimate and realizing that they know how to take things apart, but they never know how to put them back together. If they use the words "punch," "move," "add," or "eliminate," get out your checkbook.

If you need additional or replacement ceiling fixtures, don't forget track lighting. No, not your mother-in-law's track lighting! The new low-watt strips are attractive and you can hide them on the side of a beam or simply let them shine.

A warning: Get ready for many states and the federal government to enact new energy code policies regarding lighting in new and remodeled homes. In California, Title 24 aims at impacting energy consumption by incorporating lighting controls. It is especially significant in remodeling kitchens and bathrooms, since there are now requirements for using fluorescent lights. Dimmers and automatic turn-offs are required by law for other rooms in the house or apartment. As California goes on energy, so will go many other states. So be sure to check with your electrician and/or your town hall before purchasing any kind of built-in lighting fixture.

> "I refuse to endanger the health of my children in a house
> with less than three bedrooms."
>
> Myrna Loy, *Mr. Blandings Builds His Dreamhouse* (1948)

Oh, and since you are getting the electrician to do some things, have him there when the alarm company comes for its installation. You are, of course, putting in an alarm system, an affordable one that can be set off by a motion detector or a door opening.

Beds and Baths

The most important rooms in your second home are the bedrooms and bathrooms. It's logical: If this is a place to rest, you must have a comfortable place to rest your head; most people in America are used to a certain level of indoor plumbing; and, third, if you are having guests in your second home, these are the rooms that could be either the number one pleasures—or the number one problems.

First: bathrooms. You are *not* remodeling. You are *not* adding on. You have to get the bathrooms together cheaply and quickly. Recessed medicine cabinets come in fairly standard sizes and are so inexpensive at the hardware or plumbing supply stores that you never even have to think twice about scrubbing out the rust that seems a hallmark of bathrooms in recently acquired second homes. You can just pop out the old one, and pop in the new. If your house is so ancient that the measurements of the cabinet hole don't line up with any of the ready-made insert models, just buy a slightly larger-size cabinet that hangs on the wall like a framed picture. No one will know it is hiding a hole.

Find one of the attractive glass shelves that fit between the bottom of the new medicine cabinet and the faucets. They are everywhere. Target has a wide variety of cheap but chic models. Restoration Hardware has deluxe and dear ones. You have the measurements in your tote.

While you are at it, check to see if you have an electric plug close enough to the mirror, for blow-drying and shaving. If a plug is there, be sure it is a GFI safety plug. The "ground fault inter-rupter" plug shuts off the power immediately when it senses any shorting of electricity, so it is extremely important that the GFI plug be used close to sources of water, i.e., bathroom and kitchen. If there is no existing electrical plug, see if you can utilize the space behind the medicine cabinet and have the electrician run the wire to install one.

Is it better to put a toothbrush holder in the wall (remember-ing you don't know how good the plaster is) or to buy an attrac-tive and easy-to-run-through-the-dishwasher-version? Yes, you guessed it. If you don't have a big bathroom budget and the loos are already in situ in the second home, get attractive soap dishes (this is the place to use a pretty, fancy dish that you already own) and better towel racks. Or, in a small bathroom or one with lim-ited wall space, towel hooks. You can hang several hooks outside the shower, with towels ready to be grabbed. I also think that hooks allow towels to dry faster but I have no hard research on that matter.

If the second home has a shower-tub arrangement with a glass enclosure, keep the tub and ditch the glass. In a home that you will be not occupying 24-7, it is too easy to have water sit there and invite mold to come by for a long visit. Pull the glass enclosure out—carefully, as over the years the glass gets wiggly in its aluminum frame. The frame is usually held in with a couple of toggle pins, which after you remove them, leave small holes in the tile. Just fill in the small, white circular holes—or ignore them. It's an old house.

And how much fresher and cleaner to put up a curtain rod and a cheap, hip shower curtain. Shower curtains are everywhere—as are shower liners. Be prepared—even though it hurts your fingers and your back when you attach curtain and/or liner to the rings—to put up new shower-curtain liners frequently in a second home. Remember the mold—and that liner gets skanky! Plastic liners only cost around $2 each in the cheapie stores and are well worth it. Also available for about $10 are cloth liners—100 percent cotton. They are sold at linen supply stores and you can just throw them in the wash. (If you are truly frugal, you can indeed wash plastic shower-curtain liners in your washing machine.)

A perky item for your quick-fix bathroom is a bowed shower-curtain rod, available at Home Depot and Lowe's, that gives you just a little bit more room. Who hasn't felt that creepy, crawly, closed-in sense that the shower curtain is beginning to grow onto your left side? The bowed rod also makes a very nice shower curtain presentation.

In many second homes, there is only a hint of a linen closet (and you might want to use it for other storage anyway). The great solution to towel storage is the "train rack" sold by Restoration Hardware. Not cheap—they run around $200 each—but well worth the outlay, allowing you to take clean towels from the dryer directly to where they will be used. Stainless steel, some with porcelain touches, the train racks hang over the toilet and hold from six to a dozen towels, depending on the towel size and weight. One caveat: they must be put in the wall with anchors or mollies and it is a job for a handyman. Using the train racks frees up whatever is passing for a linen closet for other uses: shoes can be stored in plastic boxes, as can extra robes or sweaters or even the kids' toys.

Beds: My strong advice is to have the same kind of mattress for yourself in both your homes—easy enough with the major national chains that deliver the next day and much better for anybody with sleep problems. You will fall off quicker and easier if you don't have to readjust every time you switch houses. For guest rooms, remember, when shopping for a mattress at department stores or chain bedding stores, it is almost impossible to compare prices. Those little devils at Mattress Central never give the same name to the same style mattress sold at two separate venues. A "deluxe emperor pillow-top" in the department store could easily be a "premier restaway puff" in the mattress store. These bedding purveyors do this to confuse you and to keep you from being able to spot a real bargain. You have three ways to approach this conundrum: simply order more of what you have at home, sent to the second home address; go to a department or chain store and lie around until you find something "not too hard, not too soft"; or call or visit the mattress discount places and ask them what they have on sale on mismatched pieces. Unless you have the snoopiest guests in the world, once you put a mattress cover on, nobody will know that it doesn't match the box spring under it.

As far as bed frames are concerned, I know all about the shabby-funky door-on-its-side as a headboard. Are you mad? Do you or your family or guests want to lean up against an old door to read in bed at night? This idea is brought to you by the same folks who want you to use a door as a desk, with some handy little file cabinets to hold it up. Doors are doors.

Here is something to spend money on—an upholstered headboard. It's a quick way to spruce up any room; you can pick from tons of fabrics in catalogues (Ballard Designs is good); you can get somebody handy to make you a frame out of plywood, and get it upholstered or do it yourself (time to meet your new best friend, the staple gun); you can buy the headboards with neutral padding at almost every national furniture chain, and again, watch the sales. This is also a great recycling opportunity. Those wonderful curtains that you can't use in either house can be made into terrific headboards, as well as into matching or mixing bed skirts. But please, don't start creating duvet covers out of fancy fabric. You can't wash them. If they are silk or shiny, you can't flop on them. The best duvet covers are the cotton, sheetlike ones that you can dump in the washer—and you don't feel guilty when you discard them after a couple of seasons.

Every bedroom deserves a bookcase—or big, fat basket beside the bed to pile reading into. If you are not a serious in-the-bed-reader, but a watcher, use the bookcase or basket for DVDs or magazines.

David Mixner, my oldest friend, recently left a political and urban life for a home in the country, the perfect place to write. I know dozens of people in the movie business but no bigger fan than David. Here is his list, in no particular order, of the DVDs necessary for a second home library.

1. Víctor/Victoria
2. Tora! Tora! Tora!
3. Saving Private Ryan
4. All About Eve
5. The Women
6. Stage Door
7. Auntie Mame (the original)
8. Casablanca
9. The Godfather
10. The Sound of Music
11. What's Up, Doc?
12. Airplane
13. Chariots of Fire
14. Mrs. Miniver
15. Platoon
16. Dr. Zhivago
17. Die Hard
18. Gandhi
19. Family Guy/South Park
20. The Good Earth
21. Empire of the Sun
22. Cabaret
23. Gone with the Wind
24. The Grapes of Wrath
25. Citizen Kane
26. Shrek
27. Mary Poppins
28. Beckett
29. To Kill a Mockingbird
30. Patton
31. Hope and Glory
32. Braveheart
33. Apollo 13
34. Titanic
35. ET

And, focusing on quick fix-ups, your choice of curtains versus blinds versus nothing will depend on where your second home lives and what the outside can do to the inside. Do you need to keep the heat in or the heat out? Is the sun your friend or your foe? Are there neighbors nearby, or are the friendly woodland creatures your only observers?

As you prowl the discount stores, with your handy spiral notebook along, you will come across "panels" for window treatments. Your measurements are right with you, so you can decide if you need the 72-inch or the 84-inch or the 96-inch length, since you are not going to hem them—no, not ever. I have found the difference in the cost of panels between "furniture stores" and discount or outlet stores really remarkable. Here is a place to cut costs.

In buying drapes or panels, remember that in homes with strip heating, the heating units are usually under the windows, so you don't want anything very heavy holding *out* the heat in the winter. Of course, if you have old windows and the wind whistles through, you might need those heavy draperies to keep the house toasty. It's a toss up—and one that could land you in a place where you put window-length panels on the windows. I find this approach unusually unattractive—until I am reminded that in certain circumstances, there are no alternatives.

In very sunny climes, especially in a home you are not in and out of on a year-round basis, decisions about window covering become more complex. Sunlight will bleach anything it hits, including furniture, rugs, floors, and artwork. Unless you have been in your home or town home in various months, you have no idea where the sun hits at those various times (Earth turning on its axis and all that). There are hundreds of brands of shades, in all price categories, that promise to keep out harmful UV rays. Sheerweave gets excellent reviews and comes in many formulations and colors. Carried by many Internet sites as well as local stores, it is a good place to start your product search. It is important when shopping for shades—on the Internet, in the national hardware chains, or at a window-treatment outlet—to measure how complete the protection offered is against how much view the shades block out, especially if you are going to be using the home in a high-sun period. It's my experience that going to a higher-priced shade will give you more bang for your buck, with various "honeycomb" densities that permit more view with more protection. If that approach is outside your budget, matchstick bamboo shades in a wide variety of widths are available, again at the national hardware chains. There is also the unattractive but effective method embraced by our ancestors—use sheets to cover up anything you think might be damaged by sun. Just drape the house like Miss Haversham's living room, covering chairs, rugs, art, whatever. When you return several months later, pull off the sheets and run them through the wash.

Thinking of wash, white has its virtues and nowhere is this more apparent than with bath towels. You need one color towel for your second home and that color must be white. You can bleach white. You can use it in every bathroom (if you have more than one). You can always buy matching bath mats and shower curtains.

And it's the same with sheets. Here, it is totally up to you. You're probably going to start with sheets from your first home. Only if you are more tasteful than the rest of us will all of these sheets be white. And frequently, you will have odds and ends. Not attractive. You can pull it together by finding matelasse bedspreads. Matelasse bedspreads are the cotton covers, usually in white or cream, embossed into a design. They let you, when you are using odds and ends of sheets and pillowcases, cover the whole jumble with the spread and *voilà,* the old country-house look! These coverlets can always be found in the usual-suspect discount stores—Home Goods or Marshalls are at the top of that list—where they should run you between $30 and $50. Do not believe that there is any discernable difference between the odd-lot matelasse bedspread and the ones in the brand-name linen departments in the upscale stores.

Extra sheets for each bed get easily stored under that bed in a long, flat plastic box, making it easy for departing guests who "want to help" to make up the bed with clean sheets and bring their dirty ones to the washing machine. The matelasse also gives you the almost-instant-made-bed look, which can also be accomplished by those now-everywhere cotton quilts.

And while we are on covers, I cannot believe the variety of temperatures needed, summer and winter, to keep guests and family either cool or warm. You will need a polyester comforter or a down duvet for each bed, and a duvet cover for each, so that you can launder and not dry clean. (A duvet cover also masks errors in bedding choices you may have made along the way.) For summer use, even in a tropical clime, you need a cotton quilt or matelasse cover, especially if you are air-conditioned. I also adore afghans, in any color combinations, to perk up an all-white bed. And they keep you toasty!

A multi-choice of covers balances out what is missing in most second homes, where the luxury of multi-zone heating is not on tap. I know some people like it cold and some like it hot. I think people who want to be toasty in bed should use more covers, and not make everyone suffer in waves of warmth. It's also ecologically friendly to keep the heat down at night (and you may borrow that winning argument to counter the whining of family and friends who want to ratchet up the temperature).

3

The Kitchen

> "Well, I suppose we have to feed the Duchess. Even vultures have to eat."
>
> Shirley MacLaine, *The Children's Hour* (1961)

Looking to Be Cooking

People cook in a second home for one of two reasons: Either they love to cook, have always loved to cook and can't wait to cook—or they decide on cooking as a new avocation for this time in their life.

Whatever the motivation or rationale, cooking and its corollary, eating, are two fabulous ways to spend time in a second home. And before you get to either of those pursuits, you could also spend hundreds of hours and tens of thousands of dollars serving yourself up a new kitchen.

So, the first question about kitchens is whether or not you are

George and Barbara Thibault are our Cape Cod neighbors. They commute as many weekends as they can manage from Manhattan. George is president and CEO of the Josiah Macey Jr. Foundation, which promotes medical education for health professionals and Barbara is a historic preservationist. He is the cook; she is the sous chef and dishwasher. Their goal: "easy spontaneity." As George tells it:

I have developed the habit of keeping several meals in the freezer, so when we arrive at the beach late on Friday, we have an immediate supper, or on a lazy weekend I don't need to prepare dinner at all. The "Freezer Meals" are not just leftovers but are planned extra servings of my favorite home-cooked food. The dishes that are the best for this are lasagna, lamb stew, turkey fricassee (a turkey stew made from the leftover parts of the holiday turkey), and split-pea soup. Some meals serve two, some serve four (which might be stretched to feed five).

really going to cook in your second home. Do not go near redoing a kitchen until you decide just how much you are going to use it. If preparing meals is something you will occasionally do—between fondues or lobster rolls—or that you see as a chore rather than an adventure, don't get carried away with ranges and countertops and warming ovens. Even if you are a terrific gourmet chef, you could be coming to the mountains to ski or you would rather spend time on the sea than at the stove. Okay! You want to get by with as little kitchen, either expense or time spent in, as possible.

That does not mean, liking cooking or not, that you will be able to resist the urge to spice up your kitchen. In my world view, a remodeled or renovated kitchen is not construction. If you look at a kitchen, especially in a second home, as something you need advice on from architects and contractors and—whatever does this mean—"kitchen designers," you have missed the pride and the purpose of being a second home owner. You can hire one or all of the above, but on the whole, if you are the cook, you have to decide how it will work and do most of the work figuring it out.

The various degrees of kitchen fix-up are:

- One new appliance; or all new appliances, including a refrigerator with an ice maker; or a new stove and/or cooktop; or the addition of wall ovens; or a fan over the stove with a built-in microwave.
- New cabinets, including, if you must, new fronts for the refrigerator and the dishwasher available in styles matching the cabinets; or paint the cabinets; or remove some of them and replace them with a free-standing china closet; or put new fronts on the old cabinets; or take the doors off the old cabinets and leave them just as shelves. Being both cheap and klutzy, I have always hated those nasty little 12-inch deep, hanging kitchen cabinets that are a plague on gracious living. They are expensive and they hold nothing—especially expensive if they are new and you opt for glass fronts so you can

admire your beautiful dishes. Eliminate the middle man and go for open shelving. Your dishes can just hang right out there for people to admire without the barriers of cabinets or glass. The best-looking shelves are made with lengths of 12-inch-wide wood, finished with a nice, ready-made 2-inch bullnose. Hang them on the wall using heavy brackets. Use a lot of brackets. And try to find those wall studs. Get one of those little stud finders at the hardware store.

■ New countertops and/or a new backsplash; granite, CaesarStone, tile, laminate, man-made products of a more expensive nature like Corian, butcher block, limestone; replacing the sink with an undercounter model.

■ New countertops, cabinets, appliances, but keeping the same layout including the plumbing, electrical and flooring.

■ A walloping huge kitchen redesign with new appliances, new cabinets, new flooring, new lighting, new electrical, and new plumbing.

If that division of what you can do kitchenwise gives you a lot of choices and you thought it was simple—wait. Especially in a condo or a small home, you must spend time thinking kitchens through. In a small space, what you do *with* a kitchen is as crucial as *if* you do a kitchen. For example, the concept of a gourmet kitchen, which is what everyone wants in a primary home, with a double-size fridge and a triple-size stove with eight burners and an attached grill, is madness in a second home. If you must satisfy a hunger for all-the-rage appliances, go small and European.

There are svelte bottom-freezer refrigerators from Avanti, LG, Bosch, and Liebherr that are very *ooh-la-la* (although where those Frenchies store all their yogurt in those teensy fridges is beyond me).

You might want to check on exactly what "power sources" are available in your neck of the woods. In many country places, for example, you have electricity and the possibility of propane gas, but no natural gas. And, if you are limited to electrical ranges and cook tops, and thinking of opting for the sleek, innovative and highly rated models that heat by "magnetic power," one cost to factor in is the inability to cook with anything except stainless steel pots and pans.

Among full-size refrigerators of any brand, there is a vast difference between "freestanding" and "built-in" models. The biggest difference is price, with the built-ins running almost three times as much. The freestanders usually have a depth of 29 inches, which means they are five inches deeper than 24-inch standard cabinets. If you want cabinet-depth refrigerators, you have to opt for the built-ins. Or you can arrange your kitchen with your refrigerator adjacent to counter-topped cabinets that are built out another three or so inches. Then the fridge won't look like such a monolith. Or if you are doing more extensive work, you can carve out the wall behind the fridge and make it even out with the cabinets that way. Or you can bite the bullet and buy a built-in.

But sometimes you must have some kind of a new kitchen and you have to have one fast. Here's the good news: you can do it yourself—even in a new place without having any knowledge of local contractors or subs. Be warned: Severe cost-cutting means cutting corners as far as choices and design potential.

Chances are you are within driving distance of a Home Depot or Lowe's. Go there immediately. If you are doing other work at the house, take the contractor or the architect with you. You can tell them you are not sure if you are going to have them work on this, but it turns out you get a lot more respect in these super-sized hardware stores if you have somebody with a measure on their belt at your side. Just remember: Chatting is money. With architects and contractors, the clock is ticking and you wind up paying for their time.

If you are doing the job totally on your own, take along all the measurements of your kitchen, including windows, doors, places where the plumbing already comes out the wall, radiators, air-conditioning vents. Include any detail that can show where you can or can't put a cabinet. Spend an hour at home getting your facts and figures together. It will also serve you well to make an appointment in advance with one of the store's trained kitchen advisers.

Arrive at the supersized hardware palace of your choice a good half hour before your appointment. I am assuming that you have lived in the modern world in your primary home and so have a good idea of what things you need/want in a kitchen. Check out the various cabinet styles. I employ the Goldilocks approach with ready-made kitchen cabinets: Some are too cheap, some are too expensive, the middle-of-the-road are just right.

Once your time has arrived to meet with your kitchen adviser (the K-A), you must be conscious of the fact that not all K-As are equally trained and, beyond that, some K-As believe that their taste/style is much better than yours. The K-A is the person, however, with the computer and the ability to lay out your kitchen, so slug it through. You can also appeal to a supervisor if you any time hit an emotional/design/time problem with the K-A. Putting aside any such worries, you have several jobs to accomplish with the K-A. In order they are:

1. Pick out the cabinetmaker, the style and, in many cases, which wood—maple, oak, whatever—you want. Make the K-A really explain the differences in prices. The price list is on the K-A's computer and all of them guard it like it was a state secret. You can get a quick estimate of the cabinet cost because, even before you do the design, you know how many linear feet of bottom cabinets you need and how many uppers.

2. Using the K-A's computer and hoped-for expertise, lay out your kitchen. A caveat: If you are taller than five foot nine, make special provisions to have a base put under the lower cabinets to bring the counter level up to your height. The height of base cabinets with countertops was set decades ago at 36 inches, when Americans were considerably shorter.

3. Pick out the appliances you want, in the look you want— stainless, white, black, the same or a style similar to the cabinets; this is a chance to give your kitchen a more finished look, not by using top-of-the-line SubZeros and Vikings, but by buying all your appliances from the same manufacturer, i.e. KitchenAid, so you can get the same style

of handles, finishes, etc. Do ask if there are any specials on appliances coming up—or if the K-A could check with her manager and see if any of the floor models will be going on sale. (You can also ask if any of the sample kitchens will be sold, but that is a very rare occurrence.)

4. Pick out your sink and your faucets. Be sure to decide if you want an instant hot water (remember, you are not in this house all the time), a stainless or porcelain sink (go for a slightly better model if you choose stainless, or every time you wash a pot it will clang like a temple gong), and a single or a double sink. I had a predilection for deep single sinks until I happened on a double sink, very industrial, from Blanco. It is smashing, but it takes up a lot of potential counter space and, in most second homes, that's at a premium.

5. Pick out your countertops. This is the ultimate in personal preference. I would do without almost any home improvement to have some kind of stone countertops, be they granite or the quartz composites, CaesarStone or Silestone. My dear friend Kathy can't stand them and always does tile. The stone is obviously pricier, but tile and grout can be scum collectors. It's your money and your choice.

6. If you are going down this road truly alone, then the supersize hardware stores can provide a plumber and an electrician. You need the kitchen instantly—and they can instantly give you the skilled workmen you need.

7. If you are not doing a complete kitchen, but simply refacing—read "re-dooring"—the cabinets, try to come to

the K-A meeting with photos of your cabinets, a real measurement of each section of the cabinets, a layout of what is drawers and what is doors, and, if possible, the brand of cabinets that are already in the kitchen. You can almost always get a cabinet name from somewhere inside the cabinet. Many manufacturers put their name on the door brackets, others on the bottom of drawers. If your cabinets are so old that they precede mass manufacturing, you might want to think twice about re-dooring and just buy new—that is, unless they are solid wood. Then it might be worth your while to either buy the new doors for them—or get a carpenter to make new fronts.

8. On the cabinet front, you should have decided which cabinets are going to be used for food supply and which for dishes. For dishes, you might choose glass fronts, either in completely new cabinets or new facings—or my fave, open shelves. But, please, don't stock your pantry behind glass doors unless you are a much neater person than I.

9. Decide how to avoid the 12-inch-deep upper cabinets. They are everywhere in America and they hold so little, especially ones that are only a foot wide. Push the K-A to see if your kitchen design could include stacking two *bottom* cabinets or, if available, a 24-inch-deep top over a 24-inch-deep bottom, to create real storage place. The K-A will resist; it breaks the rules. But, especially in a teeny kitchen, an 18 or 24-inch wide by 24-inch-deep by 48 inch-high cabinet gives you huge storage for the amount of floor space it consumes. Just a thought!

Before you leave the store, get the K-A's direct phone line and also a rough idea of what days he/she is at the computer. Also, have the K-A put in writing the date when the cabinets will be ready for delivery; it will take at least several weeks. Make sure that the order specifies whether the cabinets will be delivered to your home or, if you prefer, to the store where you ordered them. Is everything included in the estimate the K-A has arrived at?

If you are using granite/stone countertops, the estimate will indeed be an estimate, since, until the cabinets are fully installed, the actual countertops cannot be measured. Then the granite/stone person will come and make a template. Then it will take at least a week, maybe a month, until your countertops arrive, and work will have to be done once the stone is at your home to make it fit exactly right. Remember, with granite or any other natural stone, it is not just what you pay for the stone, but the cost of the fabrication.

Maybe the appliances in your new second home are relatively new, but the cabinets are shabby. New fronts might make a difference, especially if you opt for a couple with framed-glass doors. Or maybe the call is whether it is worth it to bite the bullet on buying a new refrigerator, dishwasher, stove—or taking your chances on what is already there.

It's a big game of either/or which sometimes turns out to be both. It's a cautionary tale, because once you pull out those cabinets, they are gone.

Please don't let a secondhand appliance that happens to come with the house decide the eventual look or use of the kitchen. In other words, if you really want a double-door refrigerator and you will need that much storage, go ahead and get it when you do your cabinets.

Many people love IKEA. If there is an IKEA store in either of your neighborhoods, it's worth a slog through. The store has play areas and lunch areas and apparently many people make it a destination stop on the weekend. Their cabinets are sleek and come together in as many combinations as takeout pizzas. But you have to transport your purchases from the store to your home—and that could be problematic.

Everything in the store has a Nordic name—and that can be quite confusing. My husband, Bob, whose foreign language fluency is limited to ancient Greek and Latin, was sent into a paroxysm of post-teenage hysteria as we made our way through the weekend-jammed aisles during our only visit to an IKEA store. Trapped behind a large, extended family, obviously there for their routine outing, Bob became frustrated. In a Peter Sellers–like clarion voice, he created his own Nordic language, using the names of the furniture styles as nouns, verbs, adjectives, and exclamations. His speech became more rapid and excited as we rushed to the exit. Needless to say we did not go back to IKEA again.

For almost every kitchen fix-up, you will decide to change the flooring. In many second homes, especially in condos and apartments, kitchen flooring could be about as big as a doormat. If that is the case, and there are hardwood floors in other parts of the house, think about continuing hardwood into the kitchen area. With the new, prestained flooring that's available, it is considerably cheaper than the traditional method of installing a hardwood floor, avoiding sanding, staining, and sealing. Even if the rooms that border the kitchen are carpeted, prestained hardwood can be used and can really make any kitchen spiffy. If you are thinking about stone for the kitchen floor, think again. It will kill your knees. It is hard on your back. And it will destroy any piece of glass or china that you may happen to drop. On the other hand (or foot), it is good looking and easy to clean.

In an older cottage, you might come close to matching the existing hardwood floors by using the prestained material—but in a wider than the usual 3-inch width. In a warm climate, I am crazy for pre-stained bamboo. Think South Florida, Southern California, Arizona—places that you go to be warm and sunny. Nothing is sunnier than a bamboo floor, and in the 4-inch-wide stripes, it is really smashing.

Whether you do a new kitchen or make do with the old, you will need to stock and equip it. Remember that the needs of second home's kitchen are not the same as those of your primary residence. You will probably be doing quite a bit more cooking—or quite a bit less. You could be in a place with great takeout nearby—or one restaurant several miles away. And you could be buying into the barbecue culture, which I will try to restrain you from doing, but I know it is of little avail.

You don't need two of anything kitchen-wise, with a few exceptions. If there is no kitchen store handy, any decent-size supermarket should carry all of the items in the kitchen-supply box.

What You Need to Get Your Kitchen Up and Running

- The very important wine openers (plural); can openers; hot mitts, or the lovely rubber "sharks."
- Non-plastic mixing bowls (Crate & Barrel has great bright,

inexpensive stacking ones), large spoons, kitchen knives, spatulas; both a Teflon and a metal flipper; a large fork; a whisk; an eggbeater.

- A zester; a garlic press; a one-pint measuring cup; measuring spoons; kitchen scissors; a potato peeler; a meat thermometer.

- If you are planning on a lot of crowd cooking, get a good pair of poultry shears and a jumbo baster.

- Pots and pans—and this is no place to skimp. Spring for the same brand as in your primary house—you are used to cooking with them and why not!

- Cookie sheets (how else can you cook those frozen pizzas); a colander; two Pyrex lasagna-size glass pans; a large, cheap pot for boiling pasta or cooking lobsters; throw-away aluminum roasting pans.

- A coffee pot—my choice, although pricey, is the fabulous Cuisinart "Grind and Brew," eliminating the need for a coffee grinder; a toaster; a George Foreman grill; my favorite, a top-of-the-stove popcorn popper, costing about $30 and adding a real thrill to snacks; a blender and perhaps a food processor; a hand mixer.

- Glasses, in several shapes and sizes (and please look at the Reidel stemless wine glasses—the short, fat ones that can handle whites and reds and also be pressed into service for on-the-rocks drinks); Crate & Barrel has four-ounce juice glasses, some with ridges, that are the perfect size not just for juice, but for *vino Italiano*—you remember them from that little trattoria in Siena, no?

- Dishes—as many as you can store, in various patterns if

you wish, but, pretty please, make them pretty; shop the bargain stores or bring favorites from your primary house; make sure you have sufficient pasta-cereal-salad bowls (yes, use the same large bowls for all three), and if you are short on these, buy the mix-and-matching Fiesta brightly colored ones, always in stock at Bloomingdale's.

■ Napkins, cloth, but only if you promise yourself you will never, never iron them; for an extended house party, give each person an individual napkin ring, so they start with napkins fresh for dinner, and use them a second time for the next day's breakfast and it is perfectly okay that they are a little wrinkled.

You need a larder and you should remember that the main purpose of any long-term food storage is to allow you to get to your second home without stopping at a market, or to be trapped in your second home, and not have to go to the store if the weather is really nice or really nasty. You know what you enjoy. Buy it, put it on the shelves, and make sure when you finish it, you replace it. *A Twist of the Wrist: Quick Flavorful Meals with Ingredients from Jars, Cans, Bags, and Boxes*, by chef-cook-baker-restaurateur Nancy Silverton, is a great way to plan a successful pantry as well as executing delicious meals right off the cupboard shelves. (And check the box of items in my pantry!)

OATSIE'S PANTRY

Here is what is always on hand:

- Olive oil; red wine vinegar; balsamic vinegar.
- Four boxes of spaghetti; four boxes of ziti; four jars of really expensive spaghetti sauce; oatmeal.
- Jars of olives, olive paste, artichoke hearts, red and yellow peppers, cannellini beans; cans of tuna fish, salmon, and if you are that kind of person, anchovies.
- Crackers (I like the big box of Kashi from the big-box markets); popcorn; peanut butter; jam or jelly; four boxes of Pomi chopped tomatoes; two cartons of Parmalat milk (it has to be renewed every four months); two boxes of Knorr's onion soup; basmati rice mixes; dry Alessi soups; Campbell's Select soups; bouillon cubes; cereal, hot and cold.
- Hot paper cups for coffee and also some for cold drinks.
- Basic spices—thyme, rosemary, oregano, bay leaves, Old Bay Seasoning, basil, cinnamon, dry mustard, ginger, *herbs du Provençe*; condiments, including Worcestershire sauce, Tabasco, mayonnaise, yellow mustard and fancy mustard, ketchup, two small jars of chopped garlic, along with several cans of good-quality enchilada sauce and two jars of high-quality salsa.

In the freezer:

- Four boxes of brand-name creamed spinach (no, not to eat—to use as a pasta sauce with parmesan cheese); the

Continued on next page

OATSIE'S PANTRY *(continued)*

aforementioned parmesan, which came in the big bag from the wholesale stores, but which you have repacked in smaller freezer bags; two bags of broccoli florets; one pound coffee beans and one pound decaf (if you buy the vacuum-packed Starbucks from Costco or BJ's, you don't have to freeze it);

■ Two pounds of pizza dough; two packages of low-carb whole-wheat wraps; one large bag of shredded Mexican cheese mix; two pounds of high-quality ground beef; four good quality steaks or chops or chicken or those yummy New Zealand lamb chops sold in the vacuum packs at the big-box stores—whatever you like that you can defrost and have with a nice bottle of wine.

One last kitchen item—the view! If you love to cook, if you are going to really spend time cooking, then your kitchen should reflect the "I'm cooking while I'm looking" approach to design. An island that allows you to do prep while looking at the sea, the mountain, the desert sunset—that's a priceless kitchen accoutrement. If there is a possibility of the cooking-looking combo in your second home, make it happen. It will make you so happy.

4

While You're Up, Why Don't You . . .

My friend Lisa was very smart. She went to Harvard Law School, she did the *New York Times* crossword puzzle every day, even Saturday, the hardest day, and always in ink—and she served her "special pasta" to her family and friends at their second home as many times as possible.

It is the ultimate simple dish—more cutting than cooking— with the just-boiled ziti melting the teeny chunks of mozzarella and warming the pieces of tomato, all perked up by the fresh basil. You'll have to figure out the proportions yourself. I watched Lisa do it and could never quite match either her style or the taste of her dish. But it makes me feel good to make it and think of her.

If you are not using your second home to hone your kitchen skills, I am allowing you three cookbooks—a how-to-do standby, like *Joy of Cooking* or a new classic like *The Gourmet Cookbook*; a true favorite of yours from your collection; and this may surprise you, a cookbook that originates in the neighborhood of your second home. That could mean searching out a good Gulf cookbook if you are in the southern sections of Alabama, Mississippi, or the Florida Panhandle; opting for a Tex-Mex or Border-style Mexican cookbook in the Southwest; or tracking down a book featuring Cape Cod or New England cuisine if that's where you're at. Be careful not to by a locality book that is heavy on photos or on a peculiar feature of the region, i.e. just how many cranberry dishes do you want to create simply because you live near a bog?

If I bought a new cookbook, it would be *The New York Times Country Weekend Cookbook.* It has 200 recipes, from dozens of the best chefs—including sections on "make ahead salads that heat up or cool down" and an entire chapter on recipes from the farm stand.

Make it a priority and a pleasure to fall back on your old favorites. You must have something quick and easy in your repertoire already, no? How about *Marylouise's Meat Loaf?* Yes, the one with the dry onion soup is good, although I prefer Knorr's mix. Nix on breadcrumbs. I soak my cut-up bread cubes in a little milk and egg, and to really spice it up, substitute salsa for ketchup. Use any leftover veggies, also potatoes. Be adventuresome. (You can then name your meat loaf after you!)

How about my favorite *Christmas Sausages*? Chunk up red and green peppers (that's the holiday theme) along with sweet onions and cover the bottom of a baking dish with the chunks. Then cover the chunks with whole sausages—I think the hotter the better. Alternate the sausages with thick slices of Granny Smith apples, the tarter the better. Cover the whole thing with tin foil and bake at 325°F for a half hour. Take the pan out, pierce the sausages so the juice squirts out—careful, it's hot—then re-cover and cook another half hour. Uncover and cook another half hour—or until sausages are browned all around. Tasty!

Barbara Doran Sullivan is an attorney and real estate agent—and my neighbor—here on the Cape. She appeared on television for years in the 1970s, as the A&P home economist, telling us all how to use those amazing cans of cream of mushroom soup. She is a terrific cook, and with her busy life has figured out some great quickie dishes.

BARBARA'S TENNIS CASSEROLE

In a 9 x 12-baking dish combine the following ingredients:

2 pounds of stew beef, cut into cubes

4 carrots, peeled, cut into discs,

1 onion, chopped

2 celery stalks, chopped

2 bay leaves

2 cups mushrooms

1 cup red wine

1 cup beef broth

2 tablespoons tomato paste

1 tablespoons tapioca (thickening agent)

Salt and pepper to taste

Cover tightly with aluminum foil and bake in a 350°F oven for two sets of tennis. Beef should be tender and, when the match is done, so is dinner.

Serve over rice or noodles.

How about a chicken dish? Here is one I developed for a health-conscious pal. It contains almost nothing that could hurt you. *Chicken John Phillipi* is made with chicken thighs, shallots, sliced mushrooms, balsamic vinegar, random herbs—whatever you have that's green—and olive oil. Don't worry about proportions. It will all work out just fine. Cook the shallots in olive oil until soft. Dredge the chicken in the herbs, i.e. dump the herbs in a bowl and drag the thighs through. Brown the chicken on both sides in the shallots. Pour the balsamic vinegar over the thighs and scatter the uncooked mushrooms on top. Put a lid on the pan and cook about a half hour. Yum.

Or take a couple of roasters or fryers, stuff them with some lemons that you've punctured with a fork, grease them up with a little olive oil, rub in some herbs, pop them into a very hot oven for about a half hour, then turn it down until they are done. You can tell "done" by wiggling the little leg. Loose is done.

Maybe you are super at soups or stews or vegetarian wok dishes. I am mad for eggs and omelets and frittatas, and I believe that a high-point of culinary achievement is the egg salad recipe in *The Gourmet Cookbook*. Again, you could be a whiz at seafood or shrimp scampi or, lucky you, perhaps you actually know how to make a Monte Cristo sandwich. Unless you are using your second home as a place to expand your cooking repertoire or techniques, cook what you know and what you know you enjoy.

Shopping time is halved if you are doing it for an old, familiar recipe. And please don't turn your nose up at the idea of prepared foods from a local deli or restaurant. No one has to ever again prove that they can cook lasagna from scratch, or boil a lobster, or make home-made pasta, or poach a salmon. If these kinds of

My editor, *Elizabeth Beier*, totes husband, children, and piles of books to her *Columbia County* home, about two hours north of *New York*. Here's her tasty tip, courtesy of her friend *Tracy Dockray*, for an easy family and friends breakfast.

COMPANY EGGS

6 slices thick white bread, both sides buttered

2 cups grated cheese

2 cups whole milk

6 eggs, beaten slightly

Salt and pepper

1 teaspoon dry mustard

Place bread in 9x13-inch baking dish. Sprinkle with cheese.

Mix milk, eggs, and seasoning, then pour over bread. Cover and let sit, refrigerated, overnight.

Cook 350°F for 40 minutes. (Feel free to add any kind of leftovers—mushrooms, tomatoes, potatoes—but not zucchini, since it's too juicy.)

takeaway foods are good and close at hand, pick up the entree and add your own salads or desserts or fruits or whatever. And don't be embarrassed if your friends, who see you as a "really good cook," discover that you've had your good-cook ticket punched enough times at your primary house.

We must address the controversial topic of barbecue. You

might be one of the twenty-seven people in America—besides my neighbor George—who really knows how to barbecue. Good for you! For the rest of us, I most heartily recommend forgetting the coals and embracing the slow cooker, known to other generations as the Crock-Pot. A much maligned and misinterpreted wedding gift, the Crock-Pot is the answer to second home cuisine. If you are going to be out all day, lolling or antiquing or skiing or even hoisting a few over the mainsail, the Crock-Pot can be at home— think of those faithful retainers from the movies—cooking up ribs or a chuck roast, chicken, or brisket.

Buy yourself one of those cheapie Crock-Pot cookbooks in the checkout aisle of your supermarket, or even go online, if you have the need for step-by-step instructions for making cold cereal or a peanut butter sandwich. If you are a wee bit more independent, just buy a couple bottles of some semi-fancy marinade, barbecue sauce, or exotic tomato-based pasta sauce—then put whatever meat you have chosen in the Crock-Pot. (Two of my favorites are brisket and short ribs.) Then pour the some-kind-of-sauce over it, toss in some chopped up onions and potatoes, and put on the lid. Turn it on! You cannot make a mistake with a Crock-Pot. It is divine for cooking coq au vin or any kind of chicken, in any kind of sauce. Meat will be done to a fare-thee-well and nothing will taste as good as leftover brisket sandwiches, if you are lucky enough to save some brisket.

I am also mad for the George Foreman grill. It is an electronic helper that you can leave out on your kitchen counter for lunchtime grazers. It not only makes juicy hamburgers but also terrific quesadillas with the wraps and Mexican cheese, and allows you to design very yummy sandwiches with various things left over from last night's dinner. Take whatever your guests are permitted for grilled wraps or quesadillas—shredded cheese, sliced tomatoes, various cooked veggies, leftover meat—put each item in its own plastic bag, and put all the bags in a large plastic container in the refrigerator. Tell everybody where the container is. Show it to them. Tell them to be creative. It always amazes me what people will eat if they mix it up themselves.

As you are sorting out your recipes, sort out your kitchen for breakfast, lunch (as above), and dinner.

My summer kitchen is arranged so that people could—although they never absolutely do—take care of themselves for breakfast and lunch. I have one pull-out shelf supposedly designed for pots that I have instead filled with cereals, along with a handy little bagel-cutting machine called the guillotine. If I have a really full house, I try to keep jams and jellies and cream cheese in a separate container in the refrigerator—a soufflé dish works brilliantly. Then you just pop it out on the counter in the morning, pour a big pitcher of milk (so the entire half gallon doesn't get sour), and let the guests at it. Colanders with berries are good for two reasons—they always seem the right size and the fussy-pants people know the fruit is washed. My sister Jane has gifted me with several pottery "berry dishes," colander-like bowls that sit on matching saucers. Nice!

For lunch, serve the night before's leftovers (à la George Foreman), unless someone wants to drive and get lobster rolls. I also permit guests to barbecue burgers and hot dogs. I urge the use of paper plates at lunch. And paper napkins. You should buy these early in the season in great numbers—and no picking up the theme ones with yodelers or lighthouses or manatees. They are frequently very harsh and their cartoon cutesiness does not overcome their ability to shred at the touch of a ketchup dollop.

This is the absolutely simplest recipe from my pal, the Washington lobbying maven Anne Wexler, who with her husband, Joe Duffey, commutes to Sanibel each season. There, with numerous children and grandchildren in an informal compound, she wants more time for chatting than for cooking.

ANNE'S RECIPE

2 cans white beans (or fresh if you're ambitious)

1 jar Newman's Own salsa (I like either the mild or the cilantro and lime)

Chopped garlic

Lemon juice

1 to 2 pounds of fresh shrimp, either uncooked or cooked, depending on how much time you have and how many people you are feeding

1 bunch fresh cilantro, finely chopped

Put the beans (with their liquid) and the whole jar of salsa into a large pot, add the garlic, lemon juice, and half the bunch of cilantro finely chopped. Heat, add the shrimp, and cook a few minutes until the shrimp are done. Serve with fresh cilantro on top along with a crusty bread and a salad.

Voilà!

Dinner is the big challenge. Do not, repeat, do not allow someone you have never worked with to "help" you in the kitchen.
That is a recipe for disaster thought up by the Cat in the Hat. They
will spend tedious hours cutting the tomatoes up in perfect little
pieces, make some horrific strawberry and lemon salad dressing,
spill it all over their white pants so that you are doing their laundry instead of cooking dinner, and generally be a pain in the
Dutch oven. If guests or family want to be helpful they can pick
fresh flowers, water the garden, take the dog for a walk, wax the
skis, run the beach towels through the washer and dryer, skate on
the pond, take a walk to the general store to pick up ice cream
bars—or sit down and read a book.

You should, you think, be thrilled and charmed to let some
culinary-competent guest cook for you, shopping and preparing
an entire meal, especially if you have eaten at his or her home
and enjoyed their wondrous cuisine. Beware! You have no idea
how a stranger can bring havoc to your kitchen. You have no idea
how many pots and pans one cook can use, how much butter can
be burnt and left to ooze on the stove, how many knives can be
dulled, how much general carnage can be exacted by a visiting
cook. You can either cleverly have some other guest volunteer to
do the cleanup or tell yourself it's all worth it. (Guests are always
welcome, of course, to take the hosts out to lunch or dinner.)

And there is the question of desserts. The simplest, I believe, are
the ones associated with childhood memories of sweets and treats.
(This sadly would not apply to my childhood, since my parents
dragged my sister and me to various supper clubs and we special-
ized in Cherries Jubilee.) Forgetting my background, I go for ice
cream bars. Is there anything tastier than an ice cream bar on a hot

summer day? Get several styles and always opt for the expensive goopy ones. For your "presentation," get a large bowl, fill it with ice and stick the goodies in. Have another bowl of cut-up fruit for the picky contingent, and maybe some cookies. Have you ever met a cookie you didn't crave? You can always follow the recipe on the back of the Bisquick box to make cobbler if you must have something homemade or get one of those Entenmanns's frozen pound cakes, slice it, and pour on whatever is available and sweet—fruit, whipped cream, ice cream, chocolate, or caramel sauce.

In colder climes, serve up those same ice cream bars, but this time, cut them in half and plop some hot fudge on top. Yum. Or get one of the new electric fondue pots that are all over the Internet and in the gourmet stores. Don't get cultish about how you want to have the traditional flambé and fire and all that mess. The electric ones do the job and you don't char the chalet. Bananas are a universal fruit, available everywhere, as are frozen or fresh pound cakes. Chunk them both up, heat up the fudge sauce and hand out those little forks. (And you make the kids happy without standing in line at the Swiss Yodel and Fondue Café!)

If this seems too easy to be fun and tasty, it's not. People vacationing want something a little silly and sloppy, something they wouldn't dare eat or serve back at their primary homes. You can leave bars of those slice-and-bake cookies in the freezer (just be aware that the dough is delicious when chopped off in little chunks and eaten cold). Bake those little devils and shove a miniscoop of ice cream between two of them, just as they come out of the oven. Pour on a little of that hot fudge—it does come in handy, doesn't it?

I also always make sure I have packages of the silver cupcake paper liners on hand. You can make ice cream scoops earlier in

Jill Halverson, who works for Senator Jeff Bingaman and lives in Albuquerque, began her public service life in the Peace Corps. While she has served her country and her conscience well, she has also served up wonderful food over four decades. Each Fourth of July, Jill and several other Peace Corps veterans come to the Cape and introduce the exotic to what used to be just hot dogs and baked beans. Jill explains that when she lived in India in the 1960s, they ate whatever fresh food was available. And, since cauliflower and potatoes were available all winter, they had this or some variation almost every day.

2 medium boiled potatoes, cooled and diced

1 head of cauliflower, cut into florets

5 tablespoons of olive oil

1 tsp whole cumin seeds

1 teaspoon ground cumin seeds

1/2 teaspoon ground coriander seeds

1/2 teaspoon ground turmeric

1/2 teaspoon cayenne

1 Serrano chili, finely chopped

Heat the oil, when hot, add cumin seeds. Let them sizzle for a few seconds. Then add the cauliflower and stir for about 2 minutes. Cover and let the cauliflower cook for about 5 minutes. Put in the diced potatoes, the rest of the

Continued on next page

(continued from previous page)

spices and 1 teaspoon of salt and black pepper to taste. Cook until the potatoes are heated and the spices mixed. Stir carefully so as not to break up the potatoes and cauliflower. Sprinkle with chopped fresh cilantro.

the day, put them in the cupcake holders, and bring them out after dinner, piled into a mountain of ice cream balls and served with toppings. There is nothing finer than home-beaten whipped cream, with no sugar. Also yummy on brownies. Another good item to keep on hand—packages of birthday candles and maybe even some candle holders. Somebody is always celebrating a birthday, and don't you look smart that you knew about it in advance.

5

Tidy and Clean

> "No wire hangers!"
>
> Joan Crawford, *Mommie Dearest* (1981)

Closets/Storage

You already have the measurements of your various closets, written down in your second home book. Now you must make some crucial decisions: Survey your primary home closets. Not just for clothes, but for what you will copy in fixtures. (In humid climes, absolutely no metal bars are permitted, no matter what the hardware man tells you. And, again, for coat or robe hooks, try to avoid metal anything, at all costs.) You always have had those on-the floor shoe racks, but they won't work with sandals or snow boots. Maybe you should invest in plastic shoe boxes—easy to stack and, with a few cedar balls in each box, nice and fresh. How about canvas hanging bags? Go to the Container Store or Target for the best selection of these bags and bring along samples of the things you want to store in your second home—the bulky sweaters you love in winter, the pool wraps you must have in summer, one of the seventeen long-sleeve turtlenecks you cannot part with. In most second homes you are going to utilize under-the-bed or in-the-attic/basement storage and, from the beginning, you should see what size boxes do best for you. One measurement you might forget is the all-important floor-to-box-spring space, so you know how deep your storage box can be.

Only you can decide if you want a single- or double-hung closet, only you know if you need a shelf above the upper pole, and surely it is only you who knows if you and your spouse/partner will share a closet. You must make these decisions early on, since closet space is of a minimum in most second homes. If you have a guest room, perhaps you can utilize most of that closet for out-of-season clothes. Or one of you will, always self-sacrificing, agree to take that closet.

If your second home is in a hot place, will you keep anything there for cold-weather wear? And what about if you live in a hot place and commute to a second home in a colder climate, i.e. the mountains or the North Country? I don't know your answers, but I know these are questions of storage, and, sadly, storage gets handled by most people at the last minute and then there are problems.

In truly tropical climates, smart people who commute to cold places leave winter clothes in an air-conditioned room, preventing mold, nasty gnawing bugs, and decay. If you are contemplating very long stays in a hot place, with occasional airplane or train trips to cold settings, bring only the barest (no joke) minimum

John Phillips is a nationally recognized anti-fraud attorney. He and his wife, the television journalist Linda Douglass, commute between Washington, D.C.; Plymouth, Massachusetts; Buon Convento, Italy; and New York City.

One of the problems with having multiple houses is what to do about clothes in each place. Right now I have closets in four different locations. One of the benefits of having a wardrobe in each place is not having to pack a suitcase. Just get on the plane and go: no luggage or even carry-on bags. For me, this has not been a big problem because I never seem to get rid of clothes I have acquired over the years, even over decades, and now there is no way I could physically fit all of them into one of the houses. I was just observing the other day that I still had several pair of boots that were thirty-eight years old, and that they were still in great condition—so why give them up. Many of my clothes bring back memories of time and place: where I bought them; when I wore them. For example, I still have the pants I wore at my wedding—god-awful checked pants. Best of all they still fit. I even wore them to my sixtieth birthday party. They were a big hit although, as observed by all present, still god-awful. (No one could understand how I could have possibly worn such pants to my wedding!) The downside of all of this is that when we are not at our primary home, I am constantly berated by my wife for being so unstylish and uncool. It is true, but it really doesn't bother me. A friend recently

Continued on next page

(continued from previous page)

commented on my shoes, noting that he hasn't seen that style of shoe since the '70s, and the same thing with my ties, narrow, wide, very wide. I figure they all will come back in style some day and I am patient. Meanwhile, I still get good use out of them and I always try to buy good quality so they last. I did draw the line though at bell bottoms. I no longer have any, but I wonder whether I made a mistake. Could they be coming back again any year soon?

of wool with you. If you go back and forth by car, naturally you are going to need a couple changes of clothes—unless you resort to those very pungent air fresheners that taxicab drivers are so very fond of.

A very good alternative, if it is available in your locale, is the dry cleaner who will store free of charge. For the cost of cleaning each article, they will keep it in what they promise is moth-free storage, until the cold weather rolls around or until you decide to roll around to the cold weather.

More serious storage questions face you, especially in regard to memorabilia—letters, diaries, old undergraduate papers on Andy Jackson—if your second home is someplace that gets really hot and/or very humid. My friends Omar and Steve have commuted both between New York City and the country, and then finally to Florida, where they resettled. Omar's warning: "Our first house in Miami was not air-conditioned. We were on salt water

Susan Spencer *is a national correspondent for CBS and her husband, Tom Oliphant, is a political commentator and writer. They commute weekly to their farm, Fenway, in Rappahannock County, Virginia, and occasionally to their golf-adjacent dream retirement house in Arizona.*

Susan reports on both kinds of trips.

The biggest pain is the prescription drugs, and remembering to take them along. My solution is to keep several days' worth out at the farm. Then if I forget to pack them, no big deal. As far as clothes go, this is the country, so we keep tons of old, awful clothes out there, gardening stuff, roll around in the dirt stuff, stuff you wouldn't wear in public on a bet. Plus I have one pair of black pants along with about three tops, which, in a serious pinch, I could actually wear out to dinner. I can't remember the last time that happened, but by gosh, I'm ready. I also keep a pair of gray running shoes out there because you can only run on dirt roads and the white ones (the ones I wear to the swanky Ritz Carlton gym) would be wrecked in an afternoon. We go to the grocery store on the way out, so food is not an issue. We get no mail there, so we always lug the papers along; also books. Nothing is more maddening than to forget the book you're reading. We've become very adept at e-mailing ourselves. Tom writes out there a lot, I do occasionally, so we finally have this down. When the weather is nice, we pack up the cat, Veronica,

Continued on next page

(continued from previous page)

the only one of our three who actually enjoys car rides. This goes along with our philosophy that there's (almost) nothing better in bed than a nice warm cat.

As far as Tucson goes: golf clubs live there. We also have some old tennis rackets and bathing suits, along with probably three dozen T-shirts and comfortable sandals. I keep the obligatory black pants out there, too, along with a few tops, sweaters, exercise clothes, so that if I suddenly got an opportunity to go—say I had a story in Phoenix—I'd be fine. These clothes are, of course, pretty tatty by now, so I end up packing as I would for any trip. As often as I've vowed to leave things there, I find that, in the end, I can't justify leaving an outfit I really like so I can wear it only two times a year.

and everything suffered—metals rusted, furniture cracked, fabrics faded, and pictures and papers foxed like mad. In our current Fort Lauderdale house, it's less of a problem because we keep the air on all the time. No mildew, but we still manage to get crawling creatures which we just live with."

Of course they do! Do not think you are going to win when you live in a swamp. Dampness is pervasive, even if you have the air or the heat on all the time. These plagues and pests were there long before humans invented cedar closets and mothballs. I do believe strongly in DampRid, both in the hanging-bag form and in the can. Any home near water needs something in the closets that sucks up the dampness. But when you stick it in the closet, do remember that it fills up with water, so be careful when you replace it not to spill or tear that bag.

No matter how careful you are, you will lose some possessions to one of the four Miserable *M*s—Moths, Mildew, Mold, or Munching Bugs. If you are leaving a home in a hot climate for an extended period of time, you must have a friend or caretaker come through regularly and look for any or all of the Ms. And, although I don't want any place I live to be turned into a toxic waste dump, I would advise at least a couple of consultations with bug people. Ask them what they spray with and how often they spray. Look up their answers on the Internet. Most large regional or national companies are very conscious about offering somewhat safe solutions.

Cedar bags are a must for every closet in the second home, especially if you are going to be absent for long stretches of time. It is relatively inexpensive to line a closet with cedar, with strips available from Lowe's, Home Depot, or a lumber yard and costing about $200 for the material, plus labor. Or buy the small cedar blocks; stuff them into a pair of pantyhose. Hang the pantyhose on the closet bar and let the air circulate. Or use the hanging bars that are available in every location from supermarkets to linen stores. You can get several seasons out of cedar by giving it a light sanding—if you don't have any sandpaper lying about, use an emery board—when its attractive smell seems to be waning. And, on the subject of smells, be a dear and leave shoe powder in your own sneakers (which might be spending months waiting for your return) and a second container in the guest bathroom.

I am most devoted to my recently constructed cedar-lined window seat, which runs along one long wall in our bedroom. It is 18 inches high, 20 inches wide, and more than 8 feet long. Its innards store piles of stuff, and it is easy to switch winter and summer gear. But you don't have to find that much space in a bedroom. You can have someone build you a banquette in your dining or kitchen area. If your box is lined with cedar, you never have to use the smellier stuff to keep the moths away, and it can go anywhere in your second home.

I am not *sportivo*, but many people acquire second homes with the idea they are going to bike, canoe, run, ski, swim, sail, or fish. And good for them, I say. Just remember when you are putting together your fixtures and closet list to include major hooks and other hanging accessories to keep your sports accoutrements out of the way and off the floor, whether in the shed, the garage, the basement, or the coat closet. And also remember that you must, *simply must*, have a good pair of walking, gardening, hanging-out shoes that live only in the second home.

The Magic of Machines

Unless you are in a condo apartment or a teeny town house, don't even think about one of those stackable washer-dryers. Apply the Liz Taylor diamond rule to washing machines—you want the biggest one.

Your second home will be a shrine to the washable. Guests will come. They will have wash of their own. And they will contribute to the community wash! Think of the towels, linen,

Max Campion, an avid junior golfer who plays and places in national tournaments around the country, seemed the perfect person to ask about traveling with "special items." Since he's a little younger than most people with such chores, Max has some clear views on how to make this work.

Traveling with golf clubs is basically a hassle. I have a good bag, with rollers, so I can schlep around the airport. It cost like $150. But, look, even though it's sturdy, things get broken all the time. The average golfer wouldn't be lugging his or her bags that much. They would just leave them in one place—or have two sets of clubs. When a golfer is looking to buy a home, he or she has to remember that condition makes a golf course. Sure, design has a lot to do with it, but if you're playing a golf course in good condition it doesn't matter if it's on the ocean, in the mountains, on a desert, or in New England. It's all about condition.

And what is the biggest problem an avid golfer with a home on a golf course has to face?

House guests who aren't such good golfers. It's tough, because they just go and sit on the golf course.

bathrobes, pool towels, napkins, beach towels, hand towels, placemats, and yes, still more towels.

If you live alone or with a mate and you plan to never entertain, perhaps, *just perhaps,* you can get by with a stackable. My warning is to really check out the benefits and also the require-ments of the various brands. You might need a ventless dryer (which will run up the price, believe me). You might only have electric in your unit or house, which limits the options. But if stackable is all you can use, mind the brand!

Now that you are all set on getting the biggest washer–dryer combo you can possibly squeeze in, get something familiar to the repair people in your neighborhood. Maybe there is a great Swiss-Croatian washer that uses only 10 ounces of water, but you need a Swiss-Croatian to service it. Whatever. Don't buy any brand until you consult the local Yellow Pages and see that brand name on an advertisement that takes up at least a quarter of a page. (This is also a warning about using very high-end appliances in somewhat low-end locales. Before installing any of the "gourmet" brands, call the manufacturer to make sure that appropriately trained appli-ance repair people exist in your second home's part of the world.)

My washer goes constantly, in summer maybe six loads a day. People who exercise sweat. People who sit on the beach get sandy. Children fall into dirt or the lake or both. Gardening pro-duces veggies and flowers and a great number of dirty trousers and shirts. Fisherpeople come home smelling fishy. Being out-doors in any context means dirt.

I have strong feelings on laundry detergent. I have a family with skin so sensitive that the teensiest touch of strong detergent sends them screaming (especially so if they sight the aforemen-tioned cruel cleaner). So I now only buy products, such as Dreft or Arm & Hammer, which proclaim that they are safe for everybody with sensitivity.

Now, here is my exception. At least a couple times a year, I go heavy on the Clorox with the towels and then, to make sure no one gets a cranky rash, I run the towels through a second wash with just water.

One of my most precious possessions is my laundry room–pantry. In the UK they call it an airing closet, which is silly, since there are no windows. I call it salvation, since at the beach I wear a lot of things that can be washed, but not thrown into the dryer. (All of you who have shirts that "just fit" know what I mean.) Over my washer and dryer, I have a permanently installed shower curtain bar, to hang the plastic hangers on which hang all the T-shirts, white cotton pants, nighties, etc.

Forget the iron and ironing board. (I know that earlier I wrote that I had an iron, but I didn't know where it was. To be honest, I do. It is in the coat closet.) Invest in a commercial-style steamer. Heck, get one for both your homes. It will fit right beside your washer-dryer. You plug it in, heat it for a minute, and steam away. You'll look great!

Supplies

I love the way the French say cheap: *Bon marché!* I also love a bargain. And I especially love the shopping to be quick and easy, which is what you need to master to enjoy a second home. After you have made your list, here are some shopping venues for you to consider:

- **Big box stores**—such as Costco or BJ's. All bulk buying or warehouse stores require a nominal membership and, in some cases, the quantities are overwhelming. Does anybody need to buy butter in the six-pound package? Both BJ's and Costco, however, are great sources for complex cheeses, good meats, Starbucks coffee beans, as well as furniture and plumbing fixtures. You know about Costco yard furniture, but what of its amazingly lovely bathroom vanities with granite and sinks already attached. Some of these items are a little baroque for a vacation home, but you could also camp it up and stick it in the guest bathroom. Why not?

■ **Upscale jobber stores**—Marshalls, TJ Maxx, and their newest sibling, Home Goods, as well as the rougher-tougher Tuesday Morning, are not as surprisingly wonderful as they were a few years ago but are still useful. Dishes, linens, throw pillows, quilts, sheet sets, towels, candles, a scattering of furniture, rugs, kitchenware, and flatware are among the items you can find. One warning: Each of the stores might only carry a few of some prized item. I built up an entire dinner set for eighteen of Campagna dishes from Vietri, the red, white, and blue ones with the fishes. I happened upon a few in my local Home Goods and then, happily, was driving down to New York and managed to stop in at another four Home Goods until I had wiped out all available dishes, platters, mugs, and bowls in that pattern. Yes, a little time consuming but shopping fun, and my dinner service cost one-fifth of the price from a nondiscount store.

■ **Job lots**—I love 'em. I also love carnival games and funnel cakes, which fall in the same category. You have no idea what you will find in a true jobber operation; it's basically stuff that was dumped when too many were ordered by upscale stores and were then bought by a "jobber," but you knew that. Right? Some frequent purchases of mine include bath towels ($4 for ones that sold in a fancy department store for $18), myriad paper products, toasters, and mixers. I once bought sixty—that's six-oh—French cotton napkins from Tuesday Morning. I had seen similar ones, also made by Beauville, in London's Fortnum & Mason at eleven pounds each. I paid two bucks. That was almost ten years ago, and I am still using them. Frequently, the small appliances carry the warning that they are "factory reconditioned." This has to do with regulations regarding returned but unused electrical appliances, which apparently have to be rechecked before they are resold. These factory reconditioned appliances are also sold on some of the discount Web sites. Since almost everything is now made somewhere else, let me lay out my two personal prejudices: towels and bed linens from an unknown brand and dishes made in China. Too many bad stories about bath sheets with fancy-sounding labels which, after one washing, shrink into hand towels. And with the Chinese-manufactured china, it sometimes carries a warning: *not for food use*. Great, huh?

■ **Outlets**—All across America, we live close by so-called premium outlets. Villeroy & Boch have outlets everywhere, and there you will frequently find seconds or discontinued patterns. Several pals and I share the Luxembourg pattern—pretty, colorful, a Matisse on porcelain—which we all bought in a fury when it showed up in large numbers on the "discontinued" table. I called one friend who called the outlet store and bought it on the phone, and another bought it for her daughter-in-law in Florida. I gave a set as a birthday present to my pal/housecleaner Kerry, so that between us we have service for forty-plus. Other good outlets include Lenox China and Williams-Sonoma. Even Ralph Lauren has good deals on glasses, towels, and sheets in their outlet stores. Remember, there are several "classes" of Ralph Lauren, with Polo at the top and Lauren at the bottom. Ask the sales person what was the original price of anything for sale in the Ralph Lauren outlet, or you might not be getting the deal you think you are.

■ **Internet outlets**—My fave is Overstock.com, from which I have purchased hip metal dining-room chairs, armless living-room chairs, several large rugs, pillows, Criterion Collection DVDs, and my over-sized Adirondack chairs. They frequently offer $1 shipping costs as opposed to their usual $2.95. I am consistently thrilled that what I order actually shows up strongly resembling its picture and description, and if you are not happy with your purchase, they take it back. The appliances are frequently "factory reconditioned," but I think of that as a double-check. I've even bought reconditioned plasma TVs from Overstock, and they are a terrific bargain.

■ **Internet sites**—Amazon.com has a wondrous, continuously massive supply of better-quality pots and pans. I don't know why, but they do. You must search for the sale stuff, however. Sometimes the sale pots and pans won't show up unless you first put a full-price pot in your "shopping basket." Amazon becomes more and more the Internet's general store, since their umbrella now covers many smaller mom-and-pop operations. It is also, surprisingly, a great source for gourmet foods, since many smaller retailers sell through this Web site.

■ **Chain stores**—Anthropologie, the hippy-dippy clothing store, has great looking rugs and terrific drawer pulls. (Drawer pulls and knobs are so expensive in most high-end hardware-specialty stores that I think they must be made by elves.) A cool set of pulls tarts up a shabby chest of drawers. One caveat: If you are buying a secondhand chest of drawers and the drawers don't pull out easily in the antique-thrift store, they will never, never, never work. All this conversation about wax and sanding doesn't do it.

■ **Boutiques**—Beware of any local specialty store that needs too many letters to spell its name—shoppe or "beau-teak" spring to mind—or wants to show you how clever it is—consider the Kalico Kitty or the Sandy Sea Store. Such cuteness means everything costs twice as much. You are, however, encouraged to visit such enterprises at the beginning of the off-season. In most states, there are so-called inventory taxes. For a lot of start-ups, these taxes cause a problem when it's time to do the books, and this is the time when you can really do well in many smaller stores.

■ **Nearby supermarkets**—If they are part of a large chain and you have no brand loyalty, supermarkets can provide big bargains on their sales or loss leaders. I've consistently found 12-packs of soda, paper towels, detergent, and cleaning supplies that are priced better than at the big-box stores. Also, in buying supplies, you must remember that in most second homes, you are dealing with smaller spaces—unless you live in New York City, which gives new meaning to the word "cozy." It breaks my discount-devoted heart to say it, but in smaller quarters, you can too have too many paper towels.

6

Help, Help—I Have Two Houses

> "Very stupid to kill the only servant in the house. Now we
> don't even know where to find the marmalade."
>
> Judith Anderson, *And Then There Were None* (1945)

Worker Bees

How do you find someone to help you with your second home? Oh, wait! You are going to do it all yourself? Your friends and family are such cooperative people that they will strip the beds, wash the linen, remake the beds, go to the supermarket, replace the used-up supplies, and put the trash out in whatever Byzantine system your town elders decree?

(And, regarding recycling is there anything more discouraging than flunking the paper-plastic-cans test? My father avoided such problems when his frequently fly-infested Jersey Shore town cut trash collections back to once a week. A man of direct action, Ray developed the give-it-back-to-them system of trash removal. He believed that since he purchased the raw materials for trash—groceries, soda, newspapers—at a certain store, he would return the trash to that very store, dumping it either in the huge commercial cans at the store's rear or in one of the large people-friendly trash cans outside its entrance. We all lived in deadly fear that the cops would arrest him for random trash dropping, but for many, many years he skillfully avoided discovery, jauntily leaving each morning with a bag bearing the store's logo and filled with trash, and returning an hour later with a new supply of groceries.)

With trash, with cleaning, with lawns and snow and plowing roads and cutting back brush, you will sometimes need help. Finding help in a resort community is not difficult; finding help that stays with you is. If you use your second home throughout the year, or most of it, you shouldn't experience much hassle in finding someone to clean and help. If you have your home in a somewhat year-round community, and you don't use it year-round, it's a different story.

Starting at the top, you want someone to come in at least once a week during the time you are staying in the home. What you want the person to do will depend, of course, on lifestyle, time, and money—and on what you don't mind doing yourself. As the employer, you get to go first. You have several questions to answer:

- Do I mind starting with someone new each time the "season opens"?
- Do I need someone with a great deal of house-care knowledge, or just someone basically to wash windows, run the vacuum, and clean the bathrooms?

■ Is one particular house cleaner such a treasure, and
   does she/he makes my life so easy that I am willing to
   give up a lifetime of mocha lattes to keep them on? (I an-
   swered yes to that question, which is why I and not you
   have the services of Kerry of Kerry's Cleaning Service!)

■ If you are in an apartment building or a townhouse, is
   there someone available from the staff of the complex
   who can both clean for you when you are in town, and
   check on your apartment/condo when you are not? It is
   impossible, I think, to leave even a small apartment
   completely closed up for months at a time. It gets dank
   or damp or the toilet in the bathroom starts leaking or a
   window doesn't really close tight enough to keep out the
   rain. Even if you are not in a single home, you need
   someone to check in; that person could be someone already on the grounds.

Once you've hired someone, remember—you are the co-
cleaner for the first two weeks any new person starts helping
clean your house. The only way for you to measure his/her effec-
tiveness is to clean along with the person. That means you catch
the cleaner early on if you see them use the same rags on the furniture that they use on the floor; you realize that they sweep the
kitty litter under the adorable cloth you have tied around the
hundred-year-old sink; you are shocked that they don't vacuum
under the heavier furniture. (Boy, are you naive!)

You also have to have a good list of products you want them to
bring and, anytime a cleaner comes into the house, your prefer-
ences for doing certain chores. In any second home, there is a

good chance the cleaner will be doing the work mostly when you are *not* there—especially true in a weekend home. *You have to settle on how many hours versus how many chores.*

In the week following a visitor-crowded weekend, are you willing to pay for extra hours or just get the place halfway done, with the idea the cleaner will catch up the next week? That's a real concern. Be courteous and smart enough to book those extra hours in advance. If a cleaner is working for you two or four hours a week, you can be sure they are working for a lot of other people and they have to make schedule adjustments.

Be specific. Be really specific. Most cleaners have had bad experiences with clients who want the place to look like a five-star hotel, but not pay a cent to achieve the resemblance. You will have a happy and long-standing relationship with a cleaner who knows what is expected and who then can fulfill your idea of a clean house.

A caveat: Unless it is your sister and you have shared clothes since the teen years, it is impossible, on a continuing basis, to share a cleaner with a nearby neighbor. Each of you will wind up thinking the other is getting the better of the deal. Then there will come a day when you will both want the cleaner for a "special occasion" and only one will win—and that certainly will not be the cleaner.

In some resort areas, it is easy to find a cleaner in season, college kids, for example, and they are frequently cheaper than people who clean for a living. Don't be fooled. In housecleaning, you get what you pay for. And don't ever, ever, ever let anyone except the most trusted housecleaner wash your personal clothes. It is frequently not in their job description nor should it be.

In order to avoid misunderstandings and bad feelings, my

pal/housecleaner Kerry Green suggests several questions to ask a potential house cleaner:

- **Are you flexible?** For most professionals, the answer is *no*. Especially if they are cleaning for you for the six months or six weeks or the next sixteen weekends you use your second home. Don't expect a cleaning person who works alternating weeks to be able to switch this Thursday for the next, or don't assume that because you cancel out on one Tuesday that they will be able to clean the next week. "I am not on call," Kerry proclaims.
- **What will you do?** If you want a major spring cleaning—moving furniture, taking down drapes, cleaning closets—then you have to ask for and pay for a major spring cleaning. (That would be the case if you were "opening" your house after being away for several months.) If you want your house cleaned for several hours two to four times a month, then you should know it will be kitchen, bathrooms, changing beds, vacuum, and dusting. Bedding, windows, dishes, and laundry could be included or not included, but you have to work it out with your cleaner.
- **How far in advance do I need to call if I want you for extra hours?** Since a cleaner has other jobs, you can't always get—even if you are willing to pay for it—extra hours if you ask at the last minute. For a cleaner, who needs to do several houses a day, there is no way to disappoint (that's polite talk for blowing off) the next customer.

■ **How early do I have to cancel to avoid paying?** It is best to work out these details up front. Also, if you are going to be using your second home over a special holiday, a Christmas or spring vacation, find out right away if a cleaner is going to be available. Get it written down, in their calendars and yours.

■ **What do you bring with you?** Most in-and-out housekeepers bring their own equipment—vacuum cleaner and products being the two most frequent items. Find out what they use. Perhaps you have an allergy to ammonia or hate the smell of Brand-X counter cleaner. Clear up the questions now, so you don't arrive and find your place smelling like a New York taxicab, because your thoughtful cleaner put those plug-in air fresheners all over the house. Ugh!

People work for the hours you pay them for. No matter what kind of a long-term relationship you might have with your cleaning person in your primary residence, believe me, when you get to your second home, you will be entering modern times and modern rules. There is no easier way to lose a cleaner than to spend the last half hour the cleaner is there adding on more chores.

A previously employed cleaner—or one who you have kept on some kind of a retainer in the months you haven't used the house—is just who you want to get the house "opened" for the season. In olden times, when most vacation homes at the beach were unheated, when people moved to the lake for the summer, when skiing was a sport of royalty—then vacation homes didn't

get used for long periods of time. Now, admittedly, thanks to air-
planes and cheap fares, even faraway vacation homes get used
many, many months of the year.

No matter! Every house needs a big-deal sprucing up once a
year. If you have an established relationship with a cleaner, good
for you. If not, make a list of everything you want done, especially
if you won't be on the premises. Once you've made the list, go down
and check off the stuff you can do yourself once you get there. You
don't want to air out bedding but running sheets through the
washer to freshen them up isn't really onerous. When you have
pared down your list, get what you want done in written form to
the cleaner. What could be better than arriving for the season to
the smell of Lysol!

Once you have a regular cleaner committed to your house and
your schedule, you can move on to other potential helpers.

All those support systems you have built up over the years—
dependable babysitters, dog sitters, house sitters—are all far away.
Be afraid. Be very afraid. And then get organized. There are some
basic approaches for finding help, but if you think I am going to
suggest asking neighbors, I'm not. Here's why: Neighbors don't
always tell the truth.

A neighbor doesn't mean to lie, but he or she could be very
angry at one gardener for once overcharging them for weed removal; or other neighbors could be pushing a nephew who is
home for college and needs the work (and once you ask them,
they will hunt you down like a dog to hire him); or somebody will
have a semi-retired friend who doesn't really want to do gardening, but the neighbors think it will be better for him than sitting

around watching his retirement checks shrink like a cotton T-shirt. In a small town, especially, you are coming in the middle of the third act of dramas that have previously unfolded.

If you want to be successful at hiring helpers, you will have to write and follow your own script. I have some tricks for hiring help. A warning: In many resort or seasonal communities, multitasking is not a much-admired or much-acquired skill. For example, I have a wonderful lawn mower who only mows. I have a good lawn feeder. That's what he does. I have a tree man, who clips trees but not bushes.

Most single service employees turn out to provide, yes, just one service. That's what they have done for years and that is what they have chosen to do. If someone will only do one of the three tasks you need accomplished, ask him or her to refer you to a person who will do the other jobs. There are full-service landscaping businesses available for hire, but I didn't go down that garden path. I do use the full-service fellow to turn my sprinklers on and off, and to do any major bush planting. This year he put in a long strip of sea grass. And cleaned-up my rosa rugosas. Remember, many big-time landscapers offer something that a solo gardener doesn't: plant insurance. If you are planning on planting big-time, check and see if you have a one-year warranty or guarantee of replacement from whoever is doing the work.

For your regular maintenance gardener, begin by driving around the hood and seeing whose house looks best. If that gardener is too expensive (and probably will be), look for the second or third best. Try them out. It's only grass and flowers and any disaster can grow back or be replanted. Remember, hold back from any major planting until you've been in the house several months, with enough time to scope out when the sun actually hits your garden and what seems to survive best on your block.

Follow the hydrangea rule: Neighbors with large, fat flowers have been working on those bushes for eons. You can only achieve that look by throwing large, fat piles of money at the nursery and putting in full-grown plants. Also, don't make the classic new-folks mistake of trying a back-channel hire of one of the expensive landscaper's helpers. It will not work. Don't ask me how, but I know. The helper will get fired, or he will confess to his boss that he is working on the side for you and the boss will get fired up, or the neighbor who is paying full-freight for the land-scaper service will turn in both you and the helper.

(If you are going into gardening on your own, please check out chapter 12, which has even more caveats and warnings.)

When you are hiring, remember that your second home is (probably) in a small town or separated-out community and your business is always in the street.

So what listings do you need to keep the house up and running?

The names and numbers of the usual suspects—plumber, tele-phone company, cable, electrician, wood-delivery person, snow-plow person, newspaper delivery, large hauling. The telephone numbers of all nearby houses, plus the phone numbers of those neighbors in their primary homes. If it's not too pushy, you could try to scare up a couple of cell phone numbers from the neighbors.

Why, you ask. Because your neighbors, who have lived there longer, frequently know things you don't: whom to call when the trash truck doesn't show up; how strictly your community en-forces recycling; if the police respond when teenagers get drunk on the ski slope, on the town square, or on the beach; if the person with the apparently crazed dog is approachable about how little you appreciate the all-night barking, or if other people have tried and failed to shut the dog up; if there is a reasonable person to talk to on the selectman committee or city council; whether the town regularly sends out tax bills or you need to stop by city hall; whether people are going to complain if you replace windows without a permit; is the water really as drinkable as your real estate agent claimed and, if so, why is everyone else on the block getting bottled water delivered; what cell phone service actually works in this neighborhood; whether the satellite is better than the cable.

In many small towns, when you attempt to call a potential workman, someone you haven't used but have been referred to by a friend or neighbor, you will encounter the workman's dilemma: to answer—or not to answer. Okay, so when I first got to Cape Cod, I found out that many tradespeople here only answer their cell phones if they know the person calling or the number that flashes on the caller ID. And the only way to contact many of them is, you guessed it, on their cell phones. I don't know what has brought on this cultural phenomenon but here, if they don't know you, they don't give you a chance to know them.

It intrigued me. How could a painter or carpenter not answer their phone? Wasn't there possible work at the other end? Didn't matter—they just don't answer. So now I make sure that whatever worker I finally make contact with puts my number into his/her cell phone. And it's not just workers in small towns who have this approach. As I started asking other people, many of them said they followed suit, assuming that whoever was calling would leave a message or it would be a wrong number. Go figure.

And, getting more personal—how about the maintenance of you? You go to a wonderful salon just minutes from your primary home. You get your hair colored once a month. Or you have a particularly great haircut that needs a trim every three weeks. You know you have a recurring need for a little spa time. Now you're in the middle of the wild, with your hair going mad. (Maybe your "wild" is the Palm Beaches, but there you face a problem consistent in long-settled resort communities: Many people seemingly share a single vision of how blonde a blonde should be.)

It is too far—and really too silly, unless you appear regularly on television or the stage—to rush back for a touch-up or a cut, even if your primary home is just a couple hours away. You can do it, if you feel the need. For the rest of us, we're back to being fact-checkers. One approach: You see a good color job pushing carts in the veggie section of the local supermarket, but can you really go up to a woman with a ripe cantaloupe in her hand and ask her who does her hair? Sure you can. She will be complimented. Wouldn't you? If that fails, follow these approaches:

- Ask your primary colorist-stylist who he/she knows in the beauty biz in your second home neighborhood. Get your formula if you color your hair. Most stylists, knowing you won't be gone forever and happy for you to return with a full head of hair, will share their formula with you.
- Search out a salon in your second home neighborhood that uses the same products as your primary hair-care specialist. (Wow—I'm channeling a hair-care specialist just using that phrase!) Coloring products are the best

way to rate a salon far from home. My local salon, Accentuations, has top-drawer products and I found them though my neighbors. That's a two-fer!

■ Go to an upscale resort or hotel near your second home. They deal with transients all the time. If you are really nervous about what they are going to do to your hair, make an appointment for a manicure only. Check out the salon and what condition the clients are in when they check out.

■ Look for a nationally established brand-name salon. Elizabeth Arden is high on my list. There you know that the products are good, the place is clean, and the employees have been tested as to their relative competence.

I don't care if someone you know has a great budget pedicurist of some indeterminate training working out of a strip mall where the anchor store is a job lot. Don't go there! The need to have a truly sanitary place to place your footsies, especially regarding one of those high-tech bubbling chairs, should clarify that a pedicure place is not where you want to either cut a cuticle or cut back on costs.

To test a dry cleaners, send one shirt and one pair of trousers. See how they come back. More important, smell how they come back. A dry cleaner can be rated by how frequently they change the dry-cleaning fluid and the smell of old fluid is hard to miss. Don't think you will get the high-quality, high-cost couture dry cleaning that exists in big cities. There is simply not a call for it in the boondocks. But you should be able to ascertain that you can send a pretty skirt or a blazer out for dry cleaning and have it come back in decent shape. I've actually found that in many out-of-the-way places, laundry and shirts come back in superior shape than when washed by the chi-chi cosmopolitan cleaners.

To find a personal trainer, masseuse, reflexologist, or some similar rub-a-dub person, start by looking at the local health or country club. You don't have to join either to ask some questions. Do they have such full-time services? Do their service people work outside the club? (This is a good question asked face to face, when you are being really friendly to the person at the club's desk who will answer your question.) Can you contact the service person directly or are their services available only through the club? Usually the health club is tighter about allowing its staff to have independent access to a potential client and a direct payment. Country clubs, on the other hand, usually have names or references to people who might work out of the club but are not bonded to it.

7

Guests

> "If you build it, he will come."
>
> *Field of Dreams* (1989)

Wait! Make that a plural. Buy it, build it, have it—the it being a second home—and they will arrive at your door.

My sister and I grew up in a home where we never had overnight guests. Sure, we had sleepovers as kids, but the idea that friends of my parents would come and stay with us was completely out of the question. In Philadelphia, relatives were all nearby. They could drive themselves home. Anyway, our row house didn't have much spare room. At the Jersey Shore, the 1950s "Irish Riviera," we occasionally had nuns come for the day, but I can't remember anyone ever coming for an extended visit. Or even for a weekend.

So call it Freudian, but I love guests.

When I grew up and had my own house, my parents stayed

with me frequently and my father turned out to be a first-class host. Sometime during the day the guests arrived, Ray would get them to confess what kind of coffee cakes or bagels or doughnuts really made them happy; then, magically, when they came to breakfast, their favorites would be there. He also established the newspaper rule: Everyone got their very own unread paper. People love it. It makes for a lot of recycling. But there is a front page and a puzzle for each guest. Check one:

If you have a second home, you have to establish rules about guests. Check one:

❏ You will have them.
❏ You will not.

If you choose "not," skip this chapter. But let me warn you, you will be missing a lot of good times. If you are organized for guests, it's great fun.

I love those plays and films about the gracious weekend parties that enveloped Britain's country houses in the first decades of the twentieth century—even though some guests were frequently found dead in the library. Roasts and puddings and pressed linen and a personal maid to unpack you and repack you and iron you up and send you down to dinner. People organized for shoots and blundering about in Wellingtons. Or how about Hollywood, and the fabulous weekends in Palm Springs? Tennis whites and rum punch and polo mallets all around.

Did you ever notice how all those great weekender adventures seem to have a British accent? You too can acquire such élan.

Don't sneer. Some of those fusty and fancy British tricks still work. I took notes from the late Pamela Digby Haywood Churchill Harriman. (I have a pal who not only took notes, but during a Clinton inaugural party at Pamela's Georgetown home went so far as to lift up a painted garden chair to check the maker.) A renowned hostess, Pamela made everyone comfortable in her homes—not just the famous man she was might be romancing at the time. Comfort is the word. Good bedding, with reading lamps on both sides of the bed and a couple of current magazines at the ready. Nice soaps in the bathroom. So the guests are clean and well-rested . . . but what do you do with them the rest of the time?

Pamela was strict, and had a regimen for every day the guests were with her in Barbados. Breakfast was served at eight-thirty; lunch was at one, with paralyzing rum drinks a half hour before; dinner was at seven. She knew what she was doing. If you, as a host, don't give guests some boundaries, they will run over your life like invading Huns.

Have a plan and a schedule, at least for meals. Top of the list of boorish guests are those who go exploring for the day, then arrive a half hour late for the dinner you've been delaying and announce they had a scrumptious late lunch, at the very restaurant you've been dying to try.

Guests, in their attitudes and predispositions, strongly resemble toddlers. Of course they will misbehave unless they know the rules. Give them a structure, some choices of activities, the times for meals, and if the weather fails, at least a movie schedule or the location of the nearest mall.

And for the guests' sake, tell them if they need anything more than the most casual clothes. I have discovered that the further one goes from the big city, the more one goes back in time. The best restaurants in New York and Los Angeles couldn't care if you showed up in your bathrobe. Jeans are de rigueur. But get fifty miles from a freeway or subway, and suddenly you need a shirt with a collar or a sports jacket or slacks that are not made of denim. If that's the way in your second home neighborhood, be sure to tell guests before they pack.

As they unpack, let them be blown away by the charm and coziness of their room.

There are several musts for a good guest room, all of which add up to a lovely time for the guest and an easier time for you:

- A comfortable bed. Think Goldilocks—not too hard, not too soft. If you have a particular bent on beds—be it sleeping on a rock or sleeping on a cloud—don't try to convert your guests. Two pillows a person, and only one of them may be feather, and no feathers for the kids.

- Two sets of sheets for every bed. A warm comforter *and* a cotton coverlet. On the Cape, where we host people year-round, I have an old cedar chest and my cedar widow seat, both filled with all sorts of things to bundle up with, including a random selection of sweaters, afghans, and sweatshirts. People from the city come unprepared for the vagaries of waterside weather.

- Cheap cotton bathrobes, hanging on a hook on the back of the bedroom door. You can find one-size-for-all robes for, at most, $20 apiece in a discount store. They will not, sadly, fit really big people. So if you have a lot of tall or hefty folks as friends, invest in a couple of XXLs that you can track down on the Internet.

■ A chest with white shelf paper in the drawers. No scented paper, please, since some guests are allergic and some are sensibly just offended by it. There are pleasant linen sprays (Williams-Sonoma has good ones) and a quick squirt in the drawers and on the bed will make everything smell fresh and not remind you of your Aunt Betsy.

■ One of those nifty folding contraptions that hold an open suitcase. It is a self-defensive purchase, since it gives you an even chance that the guest won't open the nasty, dragged-all-over-the-world case on the crisply clean quilt.

■ In every bathroom, or in a big zip-bag in the nightstand drawer, you need some basic supplies: Band-Aids, an antibiotic cream, small tube of toothpaste, new toothbrushes, floss, nail clippers, eyebrow tweezers (for splinters), matches (for sterilizing the tweezers), toothpaste, a tube of Vaseline, a role of cotton pads, Tampax, sanitary pads, a couple of travel-size deodorants, small shampoos, a package of throwaway razors, a small can of shaving cream, a large container of liquid bath soap. By the bed, a really fancy-dancy hand/body lotion along with several bottles of water. This is no time to opt for the discount brands or finally to use up the Motel 17½ soaps and body washes. Make it lovely, and luxurious, with the exception of one bar of hypoallergenic soap.

■ A pile of good books: a couple of old and new mysteries; a few biographies; new novels; magazines. And good reading lamps, please. Everyone has a different method of falling asleep, but for a lot of people, it involves reading.

- To TV or not TV. That's your question. Do you want the guest to be able to watch the late-night talk shows or catch the early news in their room? Do you want them downstairs very late or very early? It's all up to you.

- An alarm clock and perhaps a clock radio. And a piece of paper with the house alarm code, your password, and the number of the alarm company. It will at least remind guests to try not to go out the kitchen door in the middle of the night.

- No candles—never! People occasionally drink a little too much wine when they are houseguests (since they don't have to drive home), and the last thing you need is a fire near your muslin curtains. (Candles are always a problem. Jim and Maxine, longtime figures on the political-social scene in Washington and great hosts, gave a dinner party one night, including a guest who was a just-returned-from-conflict-site diplomat. People were hanging on his every word, so he rushed in and out of the powder room, flinging a used paper towel down on the sink. Not just the sink as it turned out, but onto a lit candle—and the party became an even more flaming success.

- Especially no random candles in the desert. There temperatures can climb above one hundred for weeks in a row and you must beware candles and their ability to melt in such heat. Leave a scattering of candles on a table or sideboard and you'll return to House of Wax!

"Mother—what's the phrase—isn't quite herself today."

Tony Perkins, *Psycho* (1960)

Guest Maladies

There are two common styles of guest illnesses: those that can be helped by a visit to a doctor or the right prescription drug, and those that can be cured only by preemptive or prophylactic action by you, the host.

Nobody wants to get sick, especially not on holiday. But, as you continue to fill up your guest room, the odds are that you will wind up with a sickie.

I was at a rambunctious dinner party at a neighbor's home several summers ago, with a crowd of jolly people. My husband, Bob, arrived late and got into a spirited conversation. (Rambunctious, spirited, jolly are all code words for wine and too much food.) One woman complained to her husband that her stomach was upset and she wanted to go back to the home of the friends they were staying with. The entire table, including her husband and hosts, teased her about wanting to leave because she had too much to drink. Finally, she persuaded her party to leave a bit early. She got to their home, a short way up the road, doubled over in pain later in the night, and got to the community hospital at daybreak, just minutes before her appendix burst.

Just because you are on holiday doesn't mean something bad won't happen. If you are the host, you need to know a few things in case of the onset of a serious illness:

- What emergency services are available in your town.

- Is it a volunteer or professional fire department; are medical emergencies handled by the fire department or the police; are all firemen and/or policemen also EMTs; do you have the relevant phone numbers posted beside a phone that is convenient to everyone in the house.

- What is the expertise/quality of the nearest hospital emergency room, and does the care-quotient rise exponentially by driving another three miles to a larger, better staffed medical facility; do you have the twenty-four-hour numbers of nearby medical facilities.

- Is there a doctor or nurse at home in the immediate neighborhood; is there a fireman or an EMT close by.

- Do you have an unopened box of antihistamine pills conveniently located, just in case someone has an allergic reaction or gets a bad insect bite (spiders are notoriously evil); do you have a bottle of Benadryl for both kids and adults.

- The number of the National Poison Control Center, 1-800-222-1222, should be posted by the phone; it will immediately route your call to one of dozens of regional poison control centers.

- Also keep bottle of Ipecac handy in case a child (or adult) swallows something harmful; the child's parent, of course, is in charge and should decide whether to administer the Ipecac, which is available over the counter at any drugstore and which induces almost immediate projectile vomiting.

■ You should check with your vet as to what you should keep
  on hand if your dogs or cats get into something poisonous,
  i.e. chocolate for dogs; many vets recommend simple hy-
  drogen peroxide (Ipecac is dangerous for animals), but
  you need to find out for sure what your vet advises. Also
  refer to the Animal Poison Control Site on ASPCA.org.

Hopefully, a medical emergency won't hit. But that doesn't
mean that an occasional guest won't eat a bad mussel or crack a
molar. Your job, unless you are a doctor or a nurse, is not, never,
no way to prescribe medicine. You can and should have a selection of over-the-counter remedies on hand for your guest to
choose from. Along with the Benadryl and Ipecac, that stash
should include aspirin, ibuprofen, antacid, a tooth-numbing gel,
other antihistamines, a stop-itch stick, an Ace bandage—just
stroll down the aisles of your nearest pharmacy and stock up.
Also, if you are expecting kids, the children's version of a non-
aspirin fever-reducer and pain reliever.

If the patient seems to have picked up what we euphemistically refer to as a "stomach bug," you have to make sure—no
matter how small your hut—that they have some direct access to
and privacy in the bathroom. That also means giving them several extra wash cloths, towels, and lots of additional toilet paper
and tissues. A box of those baby wipes wouldn't be a bad idea. As
embarrassing as this might be for you, make sure there is some
kind of aerosol spray in the loo.

If they can't take a nap and awake renewed, then your ill guest
will have to be gotten home. By ill, I'm talking about someone

who has sprained an ankle, broken a wrist, gotten the flu, caught a bad cold. If he or she is traveling with a spouse, partner, or friend, you could just stick that poor soul with the responsibility. They're the ones who wanted to come to your second home and now you have other guests arriving the next day and nobody wants to wind up with Sheridan Whiteside in the best guest bedroom. Now, from several experiences with an ill guest I can tell you—they don't want to leave. You've made them comfortable, happy, soup-fed, and toasty. Why would they want to go home? Get it together and get as organized about getting them out as you were about getting them in. Help them make a plan.

If they have a rental car but are too sick, too nervous, too cranky to drive to the train or airport or back to the city, you could offer to drop off the car at the nearest rental office and help them to hire a livery service back to the city, train, or airport. If they have their own car and they live only a couple of hours away, you can try to get a neighbor or, better yet, your handyperson, to drive them home. You will ask them how they want to handle this—and even if it seems absurd and contradictory, you will bite your tongue and let them do it their way. Just get them out the door.

We had visitors once where the husband pulled his back out driving from the airport to the Cape. He was bent over in pain, but a good sport, hobbling his way through the weekend, using white wine as a crutch. Now it was time to leave, and he was going to have to get himself into the rental car, to the airport, through security, on the plane, the hour-plus flight to D.C., off the plane and into a cab, then to the doctor. I suggested a livery service, so that he would only have one transfer. His wife, a resourceful soul who spent many of her growing-up years in Europe and is not afraid of travel, knew that every transition of the trip would add extra pain. She is also frugal.

So she borrowed a pillow and quilt, plopped her husband in the reclined front seat of the medium-size rental car and drove the nine hours back to the nation's capital. Her last words to me as she pulled out of the driveway: "Does the George Washington Bridge take me to New Jersey?"

If this seems complicated, how about dealing with nonmedical guest maladies? I must admit I adore my friends and have had very few of these problems. But I have heard from other hosts. And so have you.

- **Dropsy-daisy**, where the guest leaves a book on the dining-room table, shoes beside the sofa, a wet towel on the bed, or hot rollers plugged in all day.
- **Sleeping sickness**, where the guest emerges for breakfast just as you are setting up for lunch and expects you to stay up with him or her into the wee small hours.
- **Unnoticed allergies**, where the guest suddenly announces a severe problem with being near the hair of your dog or cat.
- **Dietary delicacy**, where the guest has a yen for goat yogurt or can't eat store-bought bread or must have a certain grind of a specific brand of East African coffee.

There is a quick cure and it happens in your own head: Hey, it's my house!

If your guest's parents didn't teach politeness, you can start your pal down the right road by announcing what needs to be done. Try to work up a tone that combines Mary Poppins with Katie Couric—firm but perky. After all this visit should be a good time for all, including you.

- "Don't leave your wet towels on the bed." That's a perfectly fine thing to say to someone rude enough to do just that.
- "I'm so glad you got some extra sleep. We get up early here, so no naps for you today and an early bedtime," is another favorite.
- "Well, if you don't have your prescription with you, I have some antihistamine that seems to work wonders. And just keep your bedroom door closed, so the dogs don't get on the bed." The dogs will obviously be with you long after this pain has departed your social set.

It is up to you to give fair-warning to guests who might not know your living arrangements. Once everyone is in the house, be sure to be firm about the pet's needs. Some sample caveats: "My cat only lives *inside* the house" or "My dog will run away at the opening of the screen door."

As far as dietary wants and requests, I tell my guests that if there is something they must have, they should bring it along. Or I send out these special people to the local market and let them forage for themselves. Faced with those alternatives, you would be surprised at how few have such urgent needs.

On the whole, guests want to be good—have a good time, eat good food, be asked back. You can help guests know what is expected of them by e-mailing or faxing them an advance warning: Tell them what you have and what you don't.

A good sample is the latest version of my pre-visit note (always a work in progress):

Hi. We are waiting for you at Shrum-a-lot.

A beautiful beach and good food are on hand. There are hair dryers in every bathroom, there are robes in every closet, there are piles of good books (and if you begin one here, take it home with you to finish).

There are several brands of shampoo and lots of nice soaps and washes. The local drugstore doesn't have all the fancy labels, so pack yours if it's a life necessity. We have lots of baseball hats and a wide variety of sunscreens. We have sweatshirts for cloudy days.

If you need a broad-brimmed hat, bring it. Ditto for pool wraps. We have towels in abundance. We also have mosquito repellant. If you need a particular brand, bring it along.

If you have a child under seven—even if she is the new Esther Williams—that child must wear a real life jacket all day long whenever she is pool-adjacent or could be. We have life jackets on hand, but it's probably better if you bring along either water wings or a strap-in flotation jacket that fits your child perfectly.

If you have any special but simple dietary requirements—i.e. you need soy milk, you only eat egg-beaters, you can't stand lobster—we will try to accommodate you. Tell us what your kids eat, and if they eat with adults. If you are bringing a nanny, we need to know if she sleeps with the kids or needs her own space. Tell us now so we can be prepared.

If you are very fussy, if you use a very special tea or need to have French framboise jam on your toast to make the morning "tres jolie" or you only use the Duchess of Windsor's soap, just bring it along. You won't hurt our feelings.

We'd like to know about what time you are arriving and how you are getting here. If you are flying in or coming by train into Providence or Boston, we can refer you to Van-Go, an excellent service that will pick you up. If you are driving, Mapquest is your best guide. If you get close and are confused, that's what cell phones are made for.

We'd need to know about your exit strategy, so we can plan your last day around your timing. Again, do you need a ride, etc, etc.

We have wireless Internet service throughout the house, but we believe in the old saying that "Neither a borrower or a lender be" as regards our computers. We are both writing and live in terminal (joke!) fear of losing pages. So bring your own laptop and we can take care of you from there.

Our phone numbers:

House   Fax   Cells

Also staying with us during your visit are:

_____

And, a reminder, we do have two dogs, who spend most of the day hanging around with us and the guests. If you are allergic, bring your pills.

Can't wait to see you!

"No patty fingers if you please. The proprieties at all times."

Barry Fitzgerald, *The Quiet Man*

Sex and the Single Bed (and Other Bad Scenarios)

Birds do it. Bees do it. And so do houseguests—sometimes with a partner you were not, repeat *not*, expecting.

If you have a second home, and you have friends coming to stay, you will eventually run into one of the following scenarios:

- A recently divorced friend, man or woman, will show up with a new partner, and are so mutually enamored that the content of the day is measured on the maul scale. (They are bad guests, since they don't care about anyone else in the house; they are good guests in that their mutual fascination will keep them out of your way.)
- A couple you know well comes to visit and, zap, through the miracle of drugs, the charisma of chemistry, or the charm of your second home, they are suddenly wildly, deeply, and very passionately in love—all through the night. It's bad enough that they keep you awake; it's worse that they are so chipper in the morning you could clobber them.
- A single friend comes to stay and "links up" with a neighbor at a dinner party. For some reason, they chose your house, not the neighbor's. Suddenly, you have two lovebirds in the room with the single bed. Lucky you!

- A seemingly happy couple decides, while under your roof, to separate and then spends the weekend playing Martha and George, recounting every difference they ever had.
- A friend you thought you knew rather well shows up and goes a little weird. My best example is a middle-aged, rather stout woman acquaintance who visited at the same time as my sister and my then thirteen-year-old nephew. My sister expended a lot of energy encouraging the woman to remember to wear something over her undies when she popped out of her bedroom in the morning.
- A good friend drinks too much at Saturday lunch and continues through the afternoon and evening. Not the normal modus operandi for this pal.

All of the above scenarios are silly and simply dealt with unless you are the host. Then, your entire weekend or, even worse, week is up for grabs.

You must take charge. And you must realize that you are allowed to talk with the guest or guests about whatever hysteria they are causing. The embarrassment of erotic entanglings does not mean that you can't try to get things under control. You must, especially if there are other guests at the house.

If a relationship or marriage breaks down during a weekend, try to separate the couple as quickly as possible. If they have arrived together—via plane or car or train—you have to be resourceful. Help arrange to rent another car, or make a change in plane reservations, or do anything that is necessary to pull the sparring couple apart. Do not—unless one of them is your dearest friend in the world and seems to be in real need—offer to let one of them stay for a few days on their own. If you do, know in advance that it will be hell.

Also devilish are those people who feel just a little too at home, who want to appear in their nighties or their briefs at breakfast, telling you how well they slept. It just is not permitted. Send them back to their bedroom to put on some clothes! *Tout de suite!*

Just as quickly step in to stop someone from falling into a large glass of Merlot or a nearby snow bank or pond. You have to be firm, because booze is sometimes a bothersome side of some guests. Whatever happens, though, in your conversation with your inebriated friend, do not bring the situation to a crisis point. First, he or she could get in their car and drive away— the last thing you want to have happen. Second, if they are really in their cups, nothing you say or do is really going to matter at that moment. You will, however, have a chance in the clear light of day to explain how difficult their partying was—and you hope that they will have a great time the rest of the weekend, without making it uncomfortable for the rest of the folks at the house.

Neither a Borrower . . .

What do you do with people who want to come and visit, but you haven't issued them an invite?

It's insidious, like the first five pounds you put on after a successful diet. These guests just creep up on you. You are at a party in your primary hometown. The talk turns to second homes. Suddenly, someone you are mildly friendly with expresses an unbridled desire to visit the place where your second home is located. It can be on a beach, a lake, a golf course, a mountainside, or plunked out in the middle of the desert or the Jersey Pine Barrens. They are delighted that you have chosen this location since it is one they have always had a deep and abiding interest in. My favorite: "I've always enjoyed that part of the country. And it would be so great to have a couple weeks there to work on my book (or lesson plan or proposal or divorce or whatever)." Their enthusiasm borders on the maniacal. They are already planning their visit. Their schedule is open.

First, hold them off. Tell them you'd love to chat about the possibility of a visit, but not here, at this social occasion. Tell them to call you. They will.

Two, before that call—even if you have to stay up all night weighing the pros and cons, chatting with yourself or your partner—make a decision. If that decision is a no-go, then steel yourself to stick to it. Perhaps you find one member of the couple nerve-racking, or high maintenance, or even just boring. Perhaps you just don't want them as guests—you don't know them that well, they have an unpleasant reputation, whatever. You may have to put up with oddness and quirkiness among your family and friends, but not with acquaintances.

You are, as Nancy Reagan told America, going to just say no.

If you are a softie, you can have anyone of a series of excuses—family coming all through the season, bathrooms under reconstruction, using the second house as a place to work on your special project, red tide poisoning the beach, leeches in the lake, owls in the attic, raccoons in the basement. It doesn't matter, as long as the operative word is "no." You can be as simple as: "I went over my schedule and it won't work out this year. Let's talk in the future and see if we can make it happen."

Back to the basic concept: It is your house. And, guaranteed, unless they show up with a case of Brunello, you will have a miserable weekend. There is some reason that you've known them all these years and never gotten close.

And how about the ones who want to borrow your home?

Here's the rule. People who wouldn't ask you if they could borrow a pencil will ask to borrow your second home. Simply put, they want to be guests and they don't want you around. It's like you're giving a party and not being invited.

When they ask, you are unprepared. It's harder than staving off an unwanted guest, because this person wants your house when you don't want it—anytime you don't want it. When they ask, politeness tying your tongue into a knot, you freeze. So, before you know it, you and the person who wants to sleep in your bed and eat your provisions are, calendars in hand, making a plan to "use" your home.

They make it sound as if they will be doing you a favor by "keeping an eye on things while you are not using the house." It doesn't matter that you have neighbors, a contractor, a caretaker, and an alarm system; they are telling you that you need them. Keep their mind-set in mind as you consider this.

Lending a home is fraught with worry, based on the after-dinner horror stories of houses left in shambles, of strewn food and ski marks on the floors, of coffee-cup rings on the nightstands and dirt rings around the tub. The very idea that your haven is occupied, unsupervised, by friends or relatives provokes instantaneous fear—and sometimes loathing. You can't recall anyone ever declaring, "Wow! What a great experience. I lent my second home to friends and it was just fabulous." Still, Nancy Reagan's "no" is pretty tough, especially when dealing with family member or your spouse's best friend.

This is, however, the only way to go if you are the kind of person who is just not good at sharing. Not to be judgmental, but you could have taken a bad turn in kindergarten. Perhaps you don't share desserts, or won't lend a book, or will send dinner guests home in a sudden rainstorm, telling them they will be fine without umbrellas. If you are that person, there is no way but a polite refusal and the use of the phrase, "We never, never lend our home." I would suggest that you follow those words with something along the lines of "We'd love to have you visit when we are using the house," but that will depend if you actually are fond of these people and want to stay friends with them.

On another hand, perhaps you were happy in the past to lend your second home, but you've had a recent bad experience. If so, you now can be the kind, generous, and hearth-warming person you want to be if you set out to prepare house borrowers as well as you have prepared your home.

Remember, there are some people you can never, never lend a house to. These include anyone you think might want to throw a party and have "friends" sleep over; anyone who is devoted to their pets—they will lie and say the dog is being boarded—and anyone with small children between the ages of two and six. That last one might seem a little gruff, especially if you have little children of your own. Trust me, there will be a mess, someone will wet the bed and the rubber sheet will be forgotten, peanut butter will get ground into your rug and your kiddies' toys will be destroyed. And when you establish parameters yourself for people you would possibly lend to, be sure to share them forcefully with your spouse, partner, co-owner, or other housemate. It does no good to have it straight in your head and then have those close to you invite some variant of a Will Ferrell/Chevy Chase/Chucky characterization to move in.

Finally, to be the exception to the rule, I have had terrific experiences lending my second home. Not perfect, but terrific, especially when the person or persons I am lending the house to can really use a break.

There's a point. Anything, simply anything you have in a second home may break. And every single possession should fall into the category that if it does break, it's okay—especially in your absence. If you are lending your home, and you would die without Aunt Suzie's pie platter or a special Baccarat warthog, take the treasure off the table and stuff it into your underwear drawer.

Look around your house if it is up for lending. Remember it is not the terrible trashing of a second home that makes one-time lenders shy away from repeating the experience. It turns out that the hardest things about loaning a home are frequently the smallest things. Somebody eats that special jar of olive tapenade you saved from the holiday gift basket. Or no one put out the trash the day they left—or they put it out and didn't follow the recycling rules—so it sat there for a week. Smelly cheese was left unwrapped in the fridge. The beach towels are pristine and the bathroom towels have been to the beach.

Well, did you tell them what to do? Did you leave them a list?

I remember when I was small (and televisions were small then, too), Miss Frances of Ding Dong School had a way of putting it: Do Be a Do-Bee and Don't Be a Don't-Bee. Follow the rule of Guest-As-Toddler (only more so, because they will be unsupervised). Bring in Miss Frances and send them, before they arrive, a list of dos and don'ts.

- DO leave the house the way you find it. It will be clean when you arrive. You might think you will want to clean the house at the end of your stay. Don't even let it enter your mind. We'll arrange for our cleaning person to come in after you've left. You can leave the $____ for that service on the kitchen table. (In other words, pay up to have someone clean up.)
- DO understand what is available in the house. I am sending you our Guest Letter, detailing what we have on hand. (If you are lending a house off season, make sure they know how many quilts, coverlets, etc., you have on hand and whether the local stores are open or are keeping regular business hours.)
- DO use the washer and dryer, but understand that if you are washing beach towels or fleeces, you should be careful not to overload.
- DON'T leave any perishables behind in the refrigerator, even if you think we're coming next week. Throw out anything that goes bad. (Make a joke: We don't want secondhand food. Or maybe don't make that joke.)
- DO follow the town's recycling system. It's posted on the

wall beside the washer-dryer. If you have a large amount of actual garbage, don't leave it for the pickup. We have raccoons, coyotes, foxes, rats, mice, deer, feral cats (take your pick). Take the garbage with you, either back to the city or dispose of it at a gas station or supermarket.

■ DO leave the furniture where you found it. We like it the way we arranged it. We especially want indoor furniture left indoors, and that includes are our antique rattan and lovely twig chairs. They may look hardy; they are not.

■ DO check as soon as you arrive and make sure you see the list of emergency phone numbers by the phone in the kitchen.

Now, I am making a special point of this and you should stress this to whoever uses your house: Animals are simply not allowed. Even if you yourself are the Doctor Doolittle of the Hamptons, it's a big no. Their animals, who are acclaimed to be perfect, will "get a little excited"—that's the operative phrase—and wee on the rug. No. Bad dog!

Also, talk any house borrowers through any crankiness you may have with a certain appliance, major or minor; tell them if the coffeemaker won't work for anyone but you; and, if you have a complicated TV-in-home-theater system, you may, believe or not, tell them it is out of bounds. You can tell them it took hundreds of dollars to get it up and running, and if they must watch *Law & Order* reruns, they can do it on the TV in the guest bedroom.

Separate from but included with your e-mail or letter should be a list of the provisions you have on hand *that can be replaced easily at the nearby supermarket or store.* In addition, there is a list of specialty items that they cannot, repeat *cannot,* use—your current jar of olive tapenade from Williams-Sonoma, the cranberry chutney from your neighbor down the street, the canned tomatoes you bought in that little Italian market near your primary home, or the coffee beans in the freezer that you get by mail.

Trust me, only truffle hunting pigs can seek out delicacies faster than a house borrower! Although they are well intentioned, they will scarf down that chutney and it will be gone from your pantry forever. Again, think of Goldilocks: "This porridge was just right and she ate it all up."

So you are going to tell your borrowers just what to eat and what not to eat, and to replace any provisions that they use up. Do it with these words:

"If the coffee is *low*, or any of the other staples are *in short supply*, please replace them at the end of your stay. That way it will be all perfect when we next use the house!"

And what you probably want perfect is your bedroom. I lend my house. I don't lend my bed. Funny, since I have spent eons in hotels, but I still don't want someone else scrunching up my personal pillow. You have to decide about your pillow. If using your bedroom or your bathroom in *your* second home is something you don't want people to do—then say it! Write it! Make it clear!

Clear as vodka, perhaps. Or gin. Or one of other potables you keep on your bar or on your pantry. If there is any left. You make some sweeping statement about, "Enjoy the house," and your borrowers could be slurping up that Super Tuscan like it was tap water. So, turn off the tap. Be sure to include in your pantry list what hard liquor you have on hand that guests should feel free to drink—at long as they replenish—and where the local beer-and-wine store is located, because your wine cabinet is off-limits. You could point out that you have some very special wines—gifts from friends or bottles that are waiting for special occasions. But a total ban is the only way to insure that a Sassicaia is not replaced with a Saucy Cow.

By the way, none of these instances, complaints, or rules applies to family.

It's that simple; family first.

8

Children

Other People's

Even if you don't have children, don't know children, will never invite children or don't particularly enjoy children— read this chapter, since you will sometime have a child guest in your home.

If you have children, your tasks are mildly daunting. You must assign rooms, figuring out in some cases how many children you can squeeze into a 12 x 10-foot space without re-creating the steerage on the Mayflower. Welcome to trundle beds. You might be tempted by bunk beds, but children have a habit of growing and outgrowing the desire to sleep on the upper bunk. One exception is the very fancy designer bunk bed. I have seen photos of rooms where two large bunk-bed units are placed along one wall—and the bottom bunks actually have trundles under them. The whole arrangement sleeps six!

Anything is possible. But that doesn't mean you necessarily

want to do it. Unless you come from a very, very large family or you want to start taking in tours, a simple duet of trundle beds gives you a potential "sleeps four" situation in a normal or even smallish bedroom, yet navigable space is left because during the day only twin beds are on view.

(Understand two things: One, despite what your friends and magazine articles tell you, most children are sleeping in their parents' beds at least half the time, well, until they go to college, and almost all the time when traveling. And, two, if you put more than two children into one bedroom you geometrically increase the chances that no one will fall asleep until two A.M.)

Bed linens for younger children should consist mostly of a bottom sheet. If you are in warm weather, add a top sheet. For cooler nights, I vote for washable sleeping bags for younger kids, especially when they have sleepover friends or cousins. It makes it more adventuresome and they are not waking up at night searching for their blankets.

Some children wet the bed and it is much more terrible for them than for you. I hope that your guests will tell you if their child has that problem. If not, and there is an accident, you should have a rubber sheet nearby. Move quickly. Flip the mattress. (You will deal with whatever serious cleanup is needed the next morning. And maybe the mattress is a loss, but nothing you can do at three A.M. is going to change that.) Remake the bed as quickly as possible with the protective sheet and get the kid back into bed. Remember, the child's feelings are much more important than some piece of bedding.

In general, every child deserves one pillow, but no more, and every pillow in a child's room should be hypoallergenic. As should be any quilts or comforters. Leave the feathers and down at the door. Hypoallergenic is safer and it also makes everything machine washable.

Have videos and DVDs with Disney folks and other characters in a very specific spot, so in case of bad weather, there is something for the little visitors to do. And for goodness sake, don't get all fussy about doing the same stuff you did as a kid. Yes, jigsaw puzzles are something you remember fondly, but that doesn't mean that little Miss Techno-Wizard is going to want to spend all day on "Kittens in the Cupboard." One old reliable that does seem to work on even the most techie child is a board game. You need Chutes and Ladders for the little ones, Sorry, Rich Uncle or Monopoly for the bigger kids, and a couple editions of Trivial Pursuit for the teenagers and adults.

It's no surprise that kids love presents. I keep a laundry basket filled with the materials for instant gifts—bags, tissue paper, ribbons. Also, stick in a couple of children's books. My favorites are paperbacks of the Freddy the Pig series and Choose Your Own Adventure, neither of which are on the top of the best-seller list, but which all seem to go over well with the kiddies. Throw in some "junky" stuff, goods from the Dollar Store or the checkout counter. Light-up rings, Rubik's Cubes, joke books, comic books, old costume jewelry, pieces of Halloween costumes.

My friend Tammy Haddad is a TV producer and the most organized person in town. Good preparation, especially with kids, means good times.

Tamara Haddad, a television producer, her attorney husband Ted Greenberg, and their children Rachel and David commute between Washington, D.C., and Easton, Maryland, almost every weekend. Tammy sees their second home as the only way to escape from the minute-to-minute pressure of broadcasting—but, being a producer, she has several rules for making the ninety-minute commutes and weekends work.

■ For the car, especially in busy traffic, you need multilevel activities to keep the kids busy. That could range from playing the License Plate Game to the Beetle Game (counting the bugs) to bringing their favorite books or dolls or cars. My big trick is to bring blankets for both, so the kids can wrap themselves up, no matter the season, and feel cozy despite air-conditioning or snowy weather.

■ Give them their own backpack and put them in charge of packing it—toys, clothes, games—so they feel in charge of their world and the trip is theirs as well as yours. CDs on tape to books on tape—but never any DVDs, since arguing over which movie to watch can be a real bummer.

■ In the kid's playroom in our second house I have installed a teepee. It is the best housing investment I have ever made. As soon as we arrive, the kids immediately check it out—and that gives the adults time to unload the car.

- ■ We have a closet filled with toys, puzzles, and games for kids of all ages, so we can accommodate whoever gets there. Plastic boxes, big and small, clearly marked—crayons, paint, paper, Legos—so any kid, mine or visitors', can get exactly what they need to make them happy. And doesn't that make the adults happy!

- ■ As you come in my back door, there are coat pegs hung at a kid's height. And shoes—sneakers, boots, sandals—must be removed immediately and put in the giant closet I euphemistically call the mud room.

- ■ I have a large, plastic set of drawers on wheels. In the summer I keep pool stuff—goggles, suntan lotion, hats—in it. In the winter, I substitute all sorts of small kids stuff, so there is actually a place to put a random action figure.

For me, since I have no artistic ability and was the only girl not to get a Palmer Method Certificate for Good Penmanship in the sixth grade, there is nothing like a project. Over the years, for Halloween, I have built my son Michael into a large cardboard box (a camera), and my husband Bob into a Martello tower (several cardboard boxes). Michael was artistic and I learned that there is no better investment than a package of construction paper, some glue sticks, a large box of colored pens, and a selection of safety scissors. Tiaras, Christmas tree chains, decorated mats for photo frames, and souvenir scrapbooks are all magically created via construction paper.

Children love to make things and are amused by simple tasks. Have them draw pictures and then make the art into a book by punching holes and tying the pages together with yarn. Projects don't have to have a long shelf life, although my own mother kept shell ashtrays painted with nail polish for many, many years. But a little advance purchasing and planning can make an afternoon into a very exciting experience. Go to a stationery store and buy stickers, crayons, paints, finger paints, markers, glue, and construction paper. Who doesn't love a project?

Allow one bookshelf for visiting children. For a couple dollars each, you can build a collection of the Mr. Men and Little Miss series, i.e. Mr. Grumpy and Little Miss Giggles. Michael found these books hilarious when he was little and they seem to still hold that four-to-eight group in happy rapture. The books are inexpensive and you can send them home with the little dears. (Remember to order more!)

And don't forget about messing around in the kitchen. This is not a complicated venture with children. I've learned that almost any sandwich can be made into a "happy face" by putting the peanut butter, tuna fish, or melted cheese on half an English muffin and then adding raisin eyes and a strawberry mouth. My favorite, though, is to bake (packaged mix, please) cupcakes and then to allow the kids to slop around with frosting (green is always a winner in my house), M&Ms, sprinkles, or any other kind of gooey stuff you have that they can stick on. Kids are also a great help in making sundaes, fruit juice treats, or sticking various edible decorations on cookies and then baking them. You have the prep time and then the waiting-for-it-to-bake time and then the eating time. It is a big project that brings big results.

After you've got the little ones wired on sugar, why not play dress-up? Next time Halloween comes around, scarf up those post-holiday sale costumes. Throw them into a laundry basket, along with any really unattractive scarves, sweater, hats, Groucho Marx funny glasses, capes, odds and ends of weapons with a heavy emphasis on soft plastic swords, and all the tiaras you can get your hands on. Some inexpensive face paint is another great addition.

Your aim in all these projects is to keep the kiddies happy and busy for a short period of time. Be reasonable in your expectations. There is nothing, outside of a trip to Disneyland, that will amuse any child for an entire afternoon.

Yours, Mine and Ours

A wonderful man named Richard Hughes was governor of New Jersey in the 1960s. A widower, he met his second wife, Betty, a widow, as he was trick or treating with his four children, and she with three of her own. They married and had three children together. Years passed, and one day the governor found himself yelling, "Betty, come here. Your children and my children are fighting with our children."

In today's "melded families," there is frequently a modicum of meltdown. Yet somehow parents feel that dragging the entire combined family off to a holiday house will make it all better. I'd rip that prescription right up and try again.

Whatever the legal parameters—sole custody, weekend visitation, joint custody—when you put kids who have had two different

standards of growing-up experience in the same house, even
though everybody might want to love everybody, it gets complicated. You could translate complicated as cranky, screaming,
tantrums, hair-pulling, and/or pouting, depending on the general
personalities and ages of the children.

You are not going to work out the problems of the melded
family on holiday. But you can do certain things to ease the way
for the kids.

- Give every single child his or her own space and container. Not easy in a smaller second home, especially if
  you are utilizing bunk beds or trundles. Plastic boxes
  that sit under or beside a bed can hold the special things
  for each child—and mark each box as the sole "private
  property" of that child. Just think how you would feel if
  you were suddenly adrift, away from your "stuff"? A
  quick trip with each offspring—yes, each goes alone with
  his or her parent—to the local Bed Bath & Beyond or
  Linens-N-Things will make the bedrooms work a little
  better. Let each child and each teenager chose what they
  want. Don't worry about designs dovetailing, even if kids
  are sharing bedrooms. Let Belle live next to the Hulk.
  Children's bedrooms are about children feeling at home,
  not decorating a house.
- Even if the visit is short, unpack each child's bag and put
  their clothes away in the drawers and the closet. Nothing
  feels less permanent to a child, or an adult, than living
  out of a suitcase. You are the parent of one or more of
  these children, this is your house, and each child should

feel that it is also his or her home. My friend Kathy, now a world traveler, remembers reading about Mamie Eisenhower and how the First Lady, still an Army wife, made every government-issue apartment a home. Even if she and Ike were perching there just for a couple of weeks, she settled in, using her special dishes, unpacking and putting away all their clothes, and spreading around family photographs.

▪ Put evidence of all children on display. I remember a friend's son, who spent most of his time with the other parent, coming to visit and counting the number of photos of himself as opposed to the children of the new wife. You don't have to put your old spouse on display, but some earlier shots of you and your child, especially shots from happy times, birthday parties, or vacation trips, make it very official that this child lives here.

▪ Have things that belong to each child. If you have to ship a box with books and games or videos for each child, do it. How hard can that be?

▪ Set up some kind of a decision-making system. If there are several children and choices of activities each day—snowboarding versus skiing, biking versus swimming—either make a schedule to include each activity or—and this somehow strikes some people as strange—take your children one place and let your partner take his/her children to another. Certainly if the visit is longer than several days, take your kids out for a separate meal or outing or something. Choose them above your new partner and that family at least once or twice. Kids keep count.

- If one set of children is a regular resident at the second home, and the other set of children only rarely visits, you've got a big job on your hands. The resident kids will fight hard to defend their turf, while the visitors will try to establish a beachhead. There is no established good way to deal with any of this. Being aware is the best defense. Don't imagine that because you, your new partner, and the other set of kids find this second home wonderful that your biological children will glide right in. It just doesn't happen. Maybe you can take your kids down a few days by themselves. Maybe you can plan activities that they delight in. It becomes especially hard if the new partner's children are a whiz at the local sports—tennis, ice skating—and your kids are couch potatoes. This is no time to reprogram kids, especially ones who are holding on as best as they can. Play to their strengths, even if it's going out to a movie or visiting a bookstore.

- With teenagers, I would throw money at it. That's right. If it's only a couple of weeks, don't try to prove anything or set anyone on the right track. Give them a good time. If they live in a same state as the second home, let them take driving lessons. Or golf lessons. Try to have them do something they want to do, and if you are lucky, they will want you to do it with them. It is their vacation and you don't want to be Grizelda the Witch. This is not the time to prepare for the SATS, unless that is what they want. Movies, Chinese spareribs, gothic DVDs, spa days—satisfy their cravings. At the end of the time, let them return to their other home feeling good about their stay with you.

In General

When Marie Antoinette wanted her *bébés* to experience country life, she created a real farm right on the grounds of Versailles. (It is so good to be rich!) Cows, ducks, sheep, milkmaids—for untold sous, Marie set up Le Petit Hameau, a perfect pastoral place, bursting with the bucolic, where she could dress up as a shepherdess, and all just a quick jaunt from the main palace. *Trés jolie!*

Failing that approach, you should know what resources your second home neighborhood holds. Summer camps, craft camps, ice-skating camps—there are hundreds of possibilities and thousands of layers of sophistication and substance. Maybe this was a question you should have asked before buying your second home, and maybe you did, but now you have to figure out both the quantity and the quality of the programs available. There is a wide range and a whole list of categorical choices of camps.

- Geographically desirable. Right on your second home turf. Will they take a visiting child for a week? Do you have to sign up for the whole summer? Is everyone at the camp an expert in lifesaving and CPR? Do you have to commit to paying for the entire summer or winter holiday, or can you pay daily or weekly? Are they just a glorified babysitting service (and what's wrong with that), or will your kids learn something?
- Skill oriented. These camps are schools, or should be. A number of sports are learned by children when they are

separated from their parents. It could be golf or tennis or sailing or skiing. I think the most important judgment of such enterprises is how child oriented skill camps are. If the club pro does a once-a-week, half-hearted tennis instruction, it might be better to let the kids go over and just bat the ball around by themselves. If it is an intensive, pro-am operation, make sure it doesn't put too much pressure on your particular kiddies.

■ Team sports. Is there some objective judgment made about the child's skill level? Are previous players given preference? If it's in your town, does that move you up a notch? If you sign on as a team parent, does that increase your kid's chances of getting on the team or getting in the camp? Can you meet the coach? Okay. That's the killer. You want to make sure your precious package is in the hands of a rational human being and not someone out of a John Candy movie.

■ Do something the child wants to do. My pal Barbera has a son, Hale, who is enamored with fishing. Her father fishes and, from a small child, so has she. She spends several weeks each summer in a place where she and her preteen son go fishing. They do other things, but mostly they go fishing.

■ Individual instruction. I had a friend years ago whose son, following in the leather shoes of his lawyer father, was sports averse. He was very tall, very gangly, unable to throw a basketball—until his mother hired him a member of the first-string team from a nearby university. It was not cheap, but it made the kid confident and didn't detract one point from his massive IQ. There surely are high school or college athletes in your second home neighborhood who could be persuaded to take on a little tutelage for a little money. Learn a skill, but in private lessons. Learn to swim, to ski, to sail. Volunteer. For both boys and girls, I advance the concept of cooking lessons. Also painting lessons, even if the child shows absolutely no talent. Frame the things and put them on the wall. It's "local talent."

- Do nothing. This is the hard one, although there is simply nothing wrong with children doing nothing. You are going to have to figure out what to do with winter vacation, spring vacation, or the long hot summer with children and no program to plug them into. If they can do nothing, as opposed to whining that they want you to do something with or for them, you will be fine. Hanging out is a lost art among children and maybe yours can't do it, but they can try. Failing that, you can always send them to sleep-away camp.

9

Getting There

> "You came in that thing? You're braver than I thought."
> Carrie Fisher (as Princess Leia sighting the
> *Millennium Falcon*), Star Wars (1977)

The Chores of Traveling

According to the *New York Times*, in 2005 more than 70 percent of people who owned second homes had them in communities within one hundred miles of their primary residence. It is logical: people from Chicago go to Charlevoix or Lake Michigan, from Philadelphia to the Poconos or the Jersey Shore, from Raleigh-Durham to Duck, from Rochester to the Finger Lakes.

Despite the difference in density, vacation communities frequently take on the character of the city that is the primary residence of the majority of the resort's inhabitants. Think of Long Island beach communities as being peopled entirely by folks from

New York City and of its villages as dozens of high-rise apartments, lying on their sides.

Then think of what New Yorkers go through to get to Fire Island, where cars are banned for most of the year. Weekend com-
muters get on trains with the same amount of towage that my
grandmother had on the boat from Ireland—boxes of food and
clothing, dogs on leashes, and toddlers running amok—then transport themselves and their stuff from the train to the boat dock,
then onto the ferry and then to the island dock, where they pick
up their individual little red wagons and drag all that stuff to their
second home. Admittedly, New Yorkers are the greatest schlep-
pers in history, since even for the near rich the complications of
daily life are great and thus they master being able to get anything they own onto a subway or into a cab. Once you are there,
Fire Island seems worth it—it's just the getting there.

What is significant in the Fire Island example is that where
you make your primary residence will probably affect just
how much aggravation you will deal with in getting to your second home. (I know a Boston couple with a vacation home on a
pond fifteen minutes from their primary residence. They had
tried several other places, including Cape Cod, but they were
busy and never got to their second home. Now they do—and
they love it.)

Without a private jet, Sun Valley becomes a nightmare of
changing planes. Getting to Miami involves going through the airport located in Miami, which comes close to having Dante plan
your holiday. Unless you opt for the fifteen-minute commute, you
will find the back-and-forth taxing.

You will, even if you are superorganized, find yourself

Renowned news photographer Diana Walker and her husband, Mallory, along with an extraordinarily photogenic quartet of grandchildren, commute between Washington, D.C., and Sun Valley, Idaho. Diana is as vivid as her photos and her family embraces both the outdoor and the high-tech life with equal exuberance.

We have to remember to lug the cords to charge all that stuff we now have, i.e. cell phones, digital cameras, computers, iPods, Blackberries. We nearly need a bag dedicated to the plugs and cords! (And imagine if your second home were in Paris—yikes!) Mallory says his favorite sweater goes back and forth. He wears a particular one even though he has a pile in Ketchum. I do the same with whatever it is I am wearing a lot. It has to go with me. That goes for clothes, a favorite pair of pants and top, even eyeliner or lipstick. I am lost if I don't have the exact pencil or color.

lugging—there is no way out of it—but it becomes more manageable with some how-to-lug tips.

Federal Express and United Parcel Service have "ground service," which means it takes about five days to get a huge package across the country. FedEx has pickup boxes outside of U.S. Post Offices, but they only take up to a certain, smallish size. You can sign up for a personal FedEx account on line, at *www.fedex.com* and print out your own labels. You might have to drop larger boxes off at a FedEx store since Ground FedEx has more stringent pick-up requirements, but the preprinted label makes it faster and easier, and you are better able to access the tracking system. Once in the system, the transaction will be charged to a credit card. UPS will pick up at your house, and they are also located in Staples stores and have their own stores in many strip malls.

Shipping from a small-town post office is one of the nicest, cheapest, and easiest experiences, but don't expect service or speed from an urban post office.

Wait! You are skimming over these paragraphs, assuming you will never ship or mail anything. You will either check baggage on your plane flight or you will just leave everything in its place at your second home.

How about clothes that need dry cleaning, but you don't trust the dry cleaner near your second home? How about photo albums, or rugs, or bedding that you find you just don't need at your second home (or primary home for that matter) and want it in the other home? How about all that sports stuff that your kids seem to expend more calories toting than using? How about the summer clothes that you want to take on a Caribbean vacation during the winter? (Now that's a good one!)

The only way to travel between your homes is to make the travel part of the pleasure of owning two houses. No snickering! It is a little mind trick, sure, but once you get in the car, dogs and all, your stuff neatly in the trunk in your laundry baskets, a great CD or course on tape—how bad can that be?

If you are part of a couple, one of you will surely be the driver most of the time. It's a natural division of labor. Some people just like to drive more. In our house, it's easy; Bob gave up driving back in 1972. I once allowed him, on an early morning in 1989, to

As the executive director of the David Bohnett Foundation in Los Angeles, and despite his extensive national travel schedule, Michael Fleming tries to make it to Palm Springs every weekend with his partner, Judge Luis Lavin. As a constant traveler, Michael has strong opinions about travel to a second home.

We don't tote. Okay, maybe my laptop and a magazine from that week. But nothing else. The goal is not to tote back and forth. You lose clothes that way or things end up at the wrong house. Anything we buy in the desert stays in the desert, and that includes clothing, CDs, and books, which is perfect.

take the wheel and drive the eight blocks from our home in L.A. to pick up the Thanksgiving pies. He was like a man from Mars—he'd heard about cars, perhaps seen a photo of a car—but there was no relation between him *and* the car. In the few minutes it took us to get to the bakery, I had become embedded in the front seat. Not driving, however, does not keep Bob from navigating, a skill he excels in.

Traveling solo with pets, there is the crisis of the rest stop. If you are on a regular route between homes, and you know you or Rover will need to stop along the way, try to scope out a rest stop where there is both a relatively clean bathroom for you and some nice grass for him. I've found that in Interstate driving, it's often better to get off the highway and go into a small town, preferably one with several fast-food outlets advertised before its exit ramp. The bathrooms with be far less crowded, and the grass even greener. (And be a sport: Scoop your poop!)

Time pressures are always part of travel. To harken back again to when I lived in Los Angeles during the 1980s, people always gave the same answer when asked how long it took to get from their home to a specific destination: "Oh, about thirty-five minutes." It didn't matter if you were asking about time from San Diego to Santa Barbara. Honestly, it was always "about thirty-five minutes." That's because L.A. is a car culture and because people there are very hip and also if you said it was going to take four hours, who would do it?

Don't make yourself a prisoner of the "thirty-five-minute" standard. If you get stuck in traffic, if you leave late, if the dog throws up in the back seat and you have to stop and throw out the dog throw which is now covered with dog throw-up, it doesn't matter. The pleasure in having a second home is the pleasure of having a second home—not in getting there under "about thirty-five minutes."

If you are lucky and you have a caretaker or a neighbor, your refrigerator will contain fresh milk and bread and fruit for the morning. If you don't have such a helper, that's why elves created thermal ice chests. Take along your morning food stuffs and also maybe something nice for dinner. There is, of course, your larder and freezer and, if you are commuting back and forth, there is no reason not to stock up on chi-chi pizzas or hand-made ravioli. Something, you know, that gives you an incentive not to stop at Mickey D's. Also, make sure your freezer has a couple of plastic boxes of good leftovers, just enough for a meal for two. When I am commuting big-time, I make several meat loaves and tuck them in the back of the freezer so they don't get defrosted by a random refrigerator cruiser.

One truth is that you will have to shop in either one or both of your neighborhoods. In many cases, it will turn out that shopping near one of your homes will be a heavier chore than at the other—easier to fling cases of soda or bags of dog food into the car of your trunk in the place you have a driveway than dragging them down an urban street or through the byways of a town house community. So do your heavy shopping when you are in the easy place—or even on the way, if there is a particularly attractive market or wholesale outlet.

So now you are there, at your second home, and facing you are "chores."

No! Not now! When you arrive, only unpack perishables and what you need immediately! That is a rule I insist you keep. Get into the wonderful house, get the spouse or partner or just yourself settled, let the dog out into the backyard, and pour a glass of Chardonnay or have a cup of hot tea. The crankiness of unpacking a car and lugging stuff into a second home has been the destruction of many a great holiday or weekend.

The chores can wait until tomorrow. And, in a second home, for goodness sake, cleanliness is not next to goodliness. No way.

Those Lovable, Luggable Laundry Baskets

A laundry basket is like a good piece of jewelry—you always find a use for it. I love, *simply love,* laundry baskets. They stack up when

Geraldine and Bob Novak are committed to several endeavors outside the realm of his political column. They are devoted to their seven grandchildren and to the University of Maryland Terps, as well as to their home on Fenwick Island. Geraldine says she has made changes in commuting and toting over the years.

When we got and remodeled our latest house, starting thirteen years ago, I made sure that everything I need is already there. Cooking utensils, clothes, everything is in place, and food becomes the only decision. I keep what is in the freezer in my head. I used to cook ahead, but I have now decided that it is double or triple work, with the shopping, cooking, packing, lugging it down. Frequently I shop en route. You need a lot of choices because everyone in our family is a little bit different. One grandchild likes peanut butter and jelly, another wants buttered spaghetti. We eat at home with the children because the restaurants nearby are too crowded.

And do you and Bob listen to the Terps as you commute?

We never go when the Terps are playing. We go to the Terps.

you are not using them, they are washable, and you can see through the little holes if you can't remember what you put in the bottom.

■ Keep a laundry basket in the hall closet in each home. Stick in everything you want to go to the other house.

Marjorie Susman, a Sotheby's International representative, art collector, and social activist, shares a perfect and perfectly gorgeous but minimalist home on Nantucket with her banker husband, Louis. Their home is filled with grandchildren, children and friends.

So how far can a minimalist go?

The only thing Louis brings is a special kind of cocktail onion that he likes in his vodka. As for me, I tote a lot of strong opinions—and Louis.

Then either put the basket in the trunk of your car or lug it to UPS or FedEx for shipping.

■ Traveling with dogs or cats, keep a laundry basket in the trunk of the car with the pet equipment—a big doggie cover for the backseat; a folding cloth drinking bowl, several bottles of water, two spare leashes, and some doggie treats. With cats, you need water and treats, also whatever container you can stick the little darling into should be evened out on the slanted back seat with a pillow. Right before you leave with the pets, dump all their stuff in the backseat. And remember to remove the dogs' leashes before driving off, since they can get tangled on the dogs, the door handles, the seats—not something you want to deal with driving down I-84.

■ In summer, keep a laundry basket full of your standard summer wear, be it white cotton pants, shorts, khakis,

T-shirts, caftans, cover-ups, or sweats. Keep the basket either in the corner of your bedroom or in your bathroom, if you have the room.

■ Keep an empty laundry basket in guest room closet. Tell guests that part of the departing ritual is to bring their sheets and towels to the washer-dryer.

■ Keep another laundry basket in the bottom of the guest closet filled with bathrobes and some of the white, almost throwaway washcloths that are sold by the twenty-four-pack in the big-box stores.

■ Take several empty laundry baskets in your trunk when you go to Costco or any of the wholesale grocery stores, where they make it a principle to not only deny you shopping bags, but also to so decimate the available cardboard boxes as to make them unusable.

■ Keep a laundry basket crammed with kid stuff at your second home—puzzles or cards or easy-to-read books; crayons or paints or Silly Putty; a couple of Pixar movies or some old favorites (*Lady and the Tramp* or *Bambi*, although the dead deer do make kiddies cry).

■ Keep a laundry basket full of grown-up games like Rummikub, Scrabble, Trivial Pursuit, several decks of cards, along with some never-before-seen DVDs.

■ Keep an empty laundry basket inside or beside the outdoor shower, to keep wet beach and pool towels from traveling indoors in a drippy state.

■ In cold weather, keep a laundry basket filled with random hats and gloves and mufflers. People forget such things, especially when they come into the country. Also include sun-screen lotions and hand lotions.

■ In hot weather, keep a laundry basket filled with suntan lotions, beach hats, baseball hats, or even cover-ups. Sure, you can keep such stuff in a drawer, but it is much easier to have people rummaging around in a laundry basket for whatever they have forgotten to pack.

■ In your pantry/storage room, keep several laundry baskets on the floor or on a deep shelf. Fill one with extra plastic storage containers, plastic wrap, aluminum foil, etc.; another with paper plates, cups and disposable plastic glasses; a third with personal items, soaps, and shampoos; and a fourth with outdoor accoutrements, an apron, a long fork, tongs, the wire basket for cooking veggies on the grill, and a couple of plastic bottles of barbecue sauce (if you must).

■ Keep all insect coils and sprays in one basket and, for everyone's sake, store it high up in your coat closet, away from edibles and from the reach of children.

Not all laundry baskets are created equal. For some uses, the dorm-room-size square baskets are ideal. And just as with summer pants, white is always a perfect choice.

Abby Mandel is a "food professional"—a cookbook author, a syndicated columnist through the 1990s, and now the founder and president of Chicago's Green City Market. The market, a private charitable organization, is the only green market in the city committed to local sustainability.

Because I spend time on and off in California in the winter months only, I do one crazy thing: I ship a car out in November filled with my favorite dishes, which are no longer replaceable but I simply don't enjoy cooking/entertaining without them! This car stays for the season and brings back my dishes in May. Aside from that, I'm pretty par for the course. I pitch all basic pantry items at the end of the season due to the summer heat there. Unused wines are kept in the lowest-set refrigerator. Also, I empty the freezer.

As for double-stocking, that works for underwear, sleepwear, Gap T-shirts, jeans, sneakers, etc.—those inexpensive basics. For dressier clothes, I bring them out as I anticipate using them. I also carry makeup and medications with me.

10

Business and Bills

Keeping Track

I have three ancient smallish L. L. Bean totes, red stripes on what-was-once-white canvas, and I divide the three places I am currently living in among the three totes. In the totes are the notebooks and bits and pieces I used in putting together the house and apartments.

(Let me be clear: I lose my glasses three times a day; I forget to mail letters; I forget to write letters. All of the sorting and bagging and keeping-things-together tricks I am sharing are perfect only if you have competent and well-paid staff doing them. If you are doing them yourself, my system is a good *attempt* to hold things together.)

You might be a master of the techno universe and keep all your information on a Palm Pilot, a Blackberry, a thin-as-paper computer. And that is fine for you. I don't trust them. If you are inclined to go the electronic route, I urge you to make hard copies of your facts, and also to send your Palm Pilot info to your computer, your computer info to your Blackberry and the whole pile of information to your best friend, so when it crashes . . .

Okay, so whatever you choose as your medium of fact retention, know that you need, in each tote, notebook, or electronic device:

- A phone list that includes the numbers you need for all residences—neighbors, contractors, caretakers, plumbers, and electricians. Also every doctor's phone number and the numbers of the pharmacies in each location. I also include my insurance agent's number, and the license plate of the one car we own, which I can't ever seem to remember. Once you have that list, go to one of those copying places and have them laminate all the copies. (As soon as you do this, you will remember another number you should have on the list, but that's okay. You can do it again someday!)
- Your notebook for that particular house; photos of each room in the house (you think you remember just what color the table in the guest bedroom is, but you don't); the notebook will also contain all the measurements you took when you set up the house.
- A list of everything valuable you have in the house. That would include paintings, books, family photographs, silver salad servers, yearbooks, tuxedos, rugs, dishes.
- A list of clothing you keep in that house, or at least a list of some vital statistics, including clothes that you could wear to the city, i.e. a black handbag, black slacks, a black silk jacket, dress shirts, cuff links, a tie, leather

shoes. A friend who shares several homes with her husband told me that she had a great system of organizing—she kept a list of all her clothing in her Palm Pilot. When I asked about furniture, etc., she told me that her husband did that. What a guy!

■ A list of the products and pantry items you want to keep on hand at all times. Then, if you are going to rent or lend the house, or you are getting ready to open the house, you can tell someone else what is needed to get the place up and running; include in this list the minimum number of lightbulbs you want on hand, the wattage, and the style. You think you will remember, but you won't. Write it down.

■ A list of towels and sheets in each house. When you come upon "the greatest white sale of all time" that list allows you to restrain yourself from buying yet another set of white-with-blue-trim twin sheets when you already have four unopened sets in the closet.

■ A list of pots and pans, with a special concentration on cookie sheets, soufflé pans, and big pots. Also, it's not a bad idea to keep a count of dishes, flatware, and napkins. Again, if you are somewhere and a sale is on, you are prepared.

■ A list of appliances in each house, including kitchen appliances, radios, TVs, DVD players, heating pads, and humidifiers.

■ The art in each house. Also photos of the rugs and the curtains, along with the measurements of both. Add this to your original measurement list. Keep the list updated.

Some important measurements are the sizes of rugs, and the heights of sofas and chairs. It's good for being ready to indulge in retail therapy and also for insurance purposes.

■ A copy of your birth certificate, marriage license, passport, driver's license, etc. All of these can also be left in your underwear drawer in each house. Also, all the numbers of your various insurance policies—home, car, travel.

■ A spare copy of your prescriptions. If your doctor is fussy about this, just ask for an order for a one-month supply. It might come in handy.

The Home Office

A home office is a home office is a home office. It doesn't matter the size or placement, whether you decide that a corner of the kitchen or a corner of the bedroom is perfect. Nor does it matter if you merely need your laptop or opt for a full-scale setup with machines and two phone lines and file cabinets.

Those choices are based on preference and need up to a point. In a second home, some choices depend on the availability of tech support systems in your area, unless you feel confident enough to surf the high-tech seas solo.

■ Check out just how high-tech you can go. Stop at the nearest Staples or Office Depot and see if they've got a list of local tech-support people. Don't trust the phone book. A local business-support firm can claim that they can fix anything, and when you call, it seems the expert you need has just quit. You could also check with the nearest high school, to see if any of the computer-class instructors do any work on the side.

- Force the company that gives you high-speed computer service, phone, or cable to put in writing just how fast their service is. This is a time to ask nearby business people—law offices, real estate agents, people who use the Internet for work—what system they have installed and how it is working.

- When you put in cable and/or a high-speed Internet connection, remember that you don't have to keep the more expensive service on all year round. Many seasonal communities have a minimal off-season rate. Then you just give them a startup date for your expected return.

- Try to use the same multi-use printer/fax/copier that you have in your primary home's office. Locate the newer machine to the house where you will use it the most.

- If you are buying support machines, buy them locally. You will have a much better chance of cashing in on a warranty if you go back to the original seller.

- Think about investing in a fire-proof safe. Not too expensive, the safe will protect your passports and other valuable papers.

And where are you going to put your home office?

You need a place to work that will accommodate a high-speed hookup, a desk, and a chair. If you have guests staying with you on a regular basis, your work place can't be in the living room, the guest room, or the kitchen. So, wait! You're going to work out of the bathroom?

Flexibility in a small space goes far in creating a workable area: a laptop and a wireless system, easy to self-install, can allow you to move your "office" from the kitchen table to the bedroom to the porch, depending on how many people are sharing the house and how busy you find yourself. Make sure you copy the security code that allows access from any computer to the wireless system. Write it on a Post-It that you tape inside your desk drawer, and for good measure, add it to your emergency phone list hanging by the kitchen phone.

If you are planning on spending long periods of time in your second home, and you have a great view from a guest room or a den, don't be overly generous and save it for the guests. Take that space for yourself. It's your second home and you deserve the big picture. It's another version of "cooking and looking."

Keeping Things Up and Running

What I view as "utilities"—heat, water, alarm, gas, electric, oil, phone, cable, high-speed line, TV dish—all have regular monthly bills. These services, which seem up front and clear in your primary house, become somewhat "iffy" in your second home. It's not "if" you will get billed, but if the bill will reach you in time to pay it on time, if you will understand what the bill means, and mostly important, in a home you don't use all the time, if there is someway you can cut back.

Ellen and Robert Bennett (she's a photographer and social activist, while Bob has litigated some of America's most high-profile cases) commute during the winter months between their Washington, D.C., home and their smashing ocean-front condominium in Palm Beach. With Bob's non-stop work schedule, Ellen decided that they would travel more if they traveled light, so the apartment is outfitted with everything they need—from clothing to cosmetics, to their favorite DVDs and CDs.

"The only things I bring with me are my desk calendar, so I can make scheduling decisions, my big address book, and my prescription medications," Ellen explained.

And what does Bob bring?

"Bob brings his work."

Ummm, yes and no.

First, you do have to pay the bills. You have to find those bills, checking on whether the charge is correct, keeping track of some perhaps unnoticed detail that could skyrocket your gas or electric or cable expenses—and now you have to do it for two houses. You will be traveling back and forth between your homes and so will your vital records.

When I first acquired a true second home (as opposed to having one house under rehab while I tried to sell another), I realized that I needed a certain amount of paperwork with me at all times. That would include my checkbook, canceled checks for the past year (that's in addition to an ability to sign on to my online banking), copies of paid credit cards bills, utility bills, phone bills, copies of my insurance policies, a Xerox of my birth certificate and my marriage license, as well as the birth certificates of my husband and my grown son (be prepared), along with any construction estimates or bills.

All of this paperwork I once kept in an attractive two-drawer filing cabinet, which looked efficient, but wasn't. I then utilized a $6.95 plastic hanging-file box from Staples. It traveled back and forth in the car—but, if you travel by plane or train, the files could be packed in the USPS Priority Box and shipped ahead. The USPS Priority Box—what a great invention! A free cardboard box with a fixed postal rate of $8.10—and you can make it as heavy as you want. It doesn't change the cost.

Speaking of mail, it is best to have all the bills from both houses sent to your primary residence. This isn't as easy as it sounds; some utilities are stubbornly determined to have you receive your bill at the place you receive your service. Allow them to send the first bill to the second home, then call and have the address changed. I don't know why that works, but it does. If you inhabit your second home for several months at a stretch, i.e. summer vacation or the winter season, have your post office forward your mail. Or have a neighbor collect your mail and send it to you once a week in that fabulous USPS Priority Box.

And why not use a credit card for any bill where the company will take it? Certainly if you are on an oil heating system, a credit card is the easy way to make sure those winter deliveries keep coming. Ditto using credit cards with the phone company, which will send copies of your bills (home and cell) to your e-mail account, then you can check them out but without writing that monthly check. A mileage rewards credit card—*kazaam*!

Most banks will allow you to set up a recurring payment for mortgages or condo fees or insurance, bills which remain the same month after month. The bank will simply pay the bill on the date of the month that it is due, a date set by you. You should check on a regular basis to make sure that a hike in property taxes or insurance fees or mortgage rates has not also hiked up your monthly payments, and that you are current on these bills.

I know people out there are afraid, as I once was, of paying bills online. Try it and see if it works for you. With two houses, it saves a lot of grief.

In a two-house family, there is always concern about refilling drug prescriptions. I am very hot on keeping local businesses going, and when I lived in D.C., I was delighted to be a client of one of America's greatest drugstores, Morgan Pharmacy. They would overnight prescriptions, give good phone advice on poison ivy, on vitamins and homeopathic drugs, but they are one in a million. So now that I no longer live in D.C., I have become a captive of a mail-in prescription service. This is because I can get my refills no matter where I am. The same is true with chain drugstores, although states have different rules about what drugs can be prescribed on a quarterly basis and which can be written and filled only one month at a time. Be sure you check out the regulations on how your prescriptions work and don't just assume that you can automatically get your meds from the chain drugstore outlet near your second home.

If you are using oil to heat your home and maybe to heat your

hot water, you should check to see if the oil distributor offers a se-
nior discount or a discount if you pay within a week of receiving
the bill. Smaller, neighborhood companies frequently offer such
incentives—and you should be able to whittle down the number
of prospective oil delivery services just by checking with your
neighbors. (The exception to this rule is my home town, which has
three hundred residences and half as many different oil delivery
companies.)

11

Emergencies

> "It's easy to understand why the most beautiful poems about England were written by poets living in Italy."
>
> George Sanders, *The Ghost and Mrs. Muir* (1947)

Making a Plan

In my experience, an emergency is any time when the regular stuff just doesn't work. A hurricane, a nor'easter, a downed power line, a blizzard all qualify as emergency makers. So does an airline strike or the simple problem of your car dying in the driveway on a cold Saturday night.

If your second home gets battered by storms, wind, hurricanes, or snow, it is time to think about investing in a generator. They are not cheap but they do buy a lot of peace of mind. You'll need to decide what systems you want your generator to keep going in event of emergency: Do you want a generator that just keeps enough electricity on for the refrigerator and the thermostat, or does your partner need to have the big TV working for the duration of the storm? You can, at the time of the generator installation, even decide which lighting is necessary—be it ceiling lights or lamps—and allow power only to those circuits.

This is when you need an electrician to help you figure out what model you need. There is a huge difference in cost between generators which do enough and generators which do everything, and there are new models appearing every day. I would, however, support the slightly more expensive ones that turn on automatically when the power goes off. When you have a power outage, there is a few-seconds delay, and, *wham,* the generator turns itself on. You can tell when it happens, if you are in the house, because everything goes dark for a couple of seconds. The newest automatic models also test themselves once a month. It's amazing, isn't it, what technology can do, all by itself.

If you are alarming your home, be sure to include a "low temperature sensor" as part of your system. It is a fact that unless you drain your water system, *your pipes will burst if the water freezes.* I am amazed at how many people don't know that. With the sensor, if the temperature drops to below 40°F, a switch is tripped and it sends a signal to your alarm company. Most companies will do nothing at that point except call you and/or call the neighbor or caretaker you've designated. That's right. Alarm companies will call you about a heating problem in your house, but they will not make sure that a HVAC (heating, ventilation, air conditioning) person shows up. Unlike fire or burglary, there is, sadly, no governmental agency designated to fix your heating problem. The monitoring company is only responsible for alerting you or your backup. Also, in case of power outage, be sure the alarm company has both the number of a local contact and your cell number. If the alarm people can't reach your designated hitter, you might have a better shot yourself at finding somebody to go to your house and figure out what is happening.

Our pre-generator house was saved several winters ago when a huge storm hit Cape Cod and we were in Northern Ireland. (Rare that one feels that going to Northern Ireland can mean warmer weather, but . . .) Our neighbor, Joe, fought his way through the snow and camped out in our home, kept a fire going in the fireplace, and lit the gas burners on the stove. But such care is exceptional: A generator is the best solution.

In many older, established second home communities, there once existed a real network of retired gentlemen who were pleased to "pick up a few bucks" checking houses in the off season. Sadly, this crew is passing on and is being replaced, in many cases, by exactly nobody. So if you are counting on a caretaker to make your second home work, be advised that you should be working on the caretaker situation before you start working on the house.

You have the option of draining all the pipes in a second home that you will not use during cold weather. If you have a rustic cabin or a basic seaside cottage, and that's what you've always done—great! Of course, once you have improved a second home, you've got to measure the costs of redoing improvements (imagine refinishing hardwood floors which can buckle in the cold) against the cost of a winter's worth of heat.

Even if you are high tech, you will want an old-fashioned, hard-line phone line. Remember that any electrically powered phone system requires electrical power. That includes the chargers for cellular phones. So nothing will work without electricity, except for a phone that directly connects into the wall. In most waterside or mountainside communities, there is a real chance of power outages. So be sure to invest in a $15 phone, then plug that phone into the outlet in the spare bedroom and know that it is there. If you have opted for phone service that goes along with your cable provider, remember that when the cable goes, so does the phone service.

Whether you live in a place that doesn't usually get walloped or you have protected yourself by installing a generator, there are some very necessary steps to take. I lived for many years in Southern California and I think that maintaining an "earthquake emergency" approach is a good idea. You will probably not have the space or the basement at your second home to lay in a two weeks' supply of everything, but you should have an emergency pantry. Mine is not approved by FEMA, but let's face it, it can be a long several days until you get the power back on. Use this generalized list as a guide for your own.

- Two can openers (just in case one breaks and then where are you); cans of tuna, salmon, cat and dog food.
- A week's worth of water, some in 5-gallon plastic jugs, the rest in bottles; FEMA wants you to store one gallon of

water, per person, per day; they also want you to store at
least a two-week supply for each member of your family.
That translates, for each person in your family, to three
5-gallon jugs. That's a lot of water, and most emergencies don't last that long. But after we've seen what happened with Katrina, we should all be considering how
much water we need to safely get through.

- Paper products, including plates, cups, paper towels, toilet paper, trash bags; a large cooler.

- Duct tape and heavy-duty green trash bags (so you can
tape up any windows that may break).

- Flashlights, the all-too-great flashlight lamps, and unopened packages of AAA, AA, and D batteries, just in
case.

- Three good bottles of wine, two wine openers, crackers,
peanut butter, jars of fancy olive, artichoke, and pimiento
spread; breakfast bars; if you are a coffeeholic, get a six-
pack of Starbucks Frappuccinos (it might not be just the
way you order it, but it is coffee); three dozen packets of
mayonnaise (you can pick them up the next time you are
in a fast-food place), ditto for mustard.

- For the kids: cereal, Parmalat milk with the months-long
shelf life; crackers, pretzels, dried fruit, cookies in small
bags, canned fruit.

- Kitty litter, spare leashes, a fold-up cat carrier, pet food.

- Very important: cash. ATMs don't work when the power
goes out. You might decide to avoid a storm by getting
out of town, and you'll need dollars. (If your second

home is in another country, you need both dollars and the local currency.) Keep the cash somewhere with your emergency supplies (or, of course, in your underwear drawer).

- Even if you are not a game player, make sure you have a Scrabble or a Rummikub somewhere in the house. Several days without television is a long, long time.
- A good battery-operated radio, one that hopefully will also pick up weather forecasts. Any of the gadget stores— Sharper Image, Radio Shack —will have these, as will travel stores.
- If you have a wood fireplace, heat should not be a problem. Throw several of those Duralogs into your emergency pantry, just in case you forgot to get wood. And a bag of marshmallows. Always festive.

Remember, if the power goes out and you think it will be restored shortly, do not open your refrigerator. Food inside will stay fresh, according to my food-safety-consultant neighbor Carol Mier, for at least twenty-four hours. If you know of a storm in advance and are riding it out, spend a little time loading up your freezer with cooked food. The tuna gets tired after a day, but how about some nice flank steak, eh?

Here's another great tip from Carol: If you are in danger of evacuation, you can pack a seventy-two-hour emergency food kit into a half-gallon cardboard orange juice container. (I know. It's like making furniture from seashells, but no, this works.) Wash and dry the cardboard container. Pack, in this order:

Two pull-top cans of Vienna sausage, two packages of peanut butter Crackers, two granola bars, two packets of hot chocolate, two packets instant oatmeal, one oatmeal square, one small can fruit, one bag trail mix, two beef jerky sticks, one plastic spoon, nine pieces of small hard candy. Carol also has a sample menu, but you can figure it out. Each cardboard container feeds one person for three days. And assembling it is a great activity for kids or guests on a rainy day when they have gotten bored with Scrabble.

BJs, Home Depot, Costco, and Lowe's, along with many others, sell a great battery-operated lamp that resembles a kerosene hurricane lamp. It throws off a lot of light, it is cheap and you can leave it on a bookshelf (as opposed to a flashlight, which will migrate around the house and eventually just disappear). Not just for emergencies, but for every day, keep a good supply of batteries in a second house. Although old wives say to keep them in the refrigerator, the only reason I can understand doing that is if you live in a really hot, hot climate.

Whatever you plan to do to deal with an emergency, do make a plan. Part of any emergency plan should be the way you deal with avoiding emergencies in your day-to-day running of the house. Whether you have a seasoned contractor or a casual caretaker, there are certain maintenance issues that you might check on yourself.

■ Away from the big city, or the suburb, there is our friend, the septic system. And that septic requires maintenance every several years. No, I can't be more specific, because

I don't know how much you use it. You should chat with your septic-cleaning service. And you should make a decision, with them, about using products such as Rid-X to clean your septic system between pumping. There is a question as to whether interfering with the bacteria slows down or speeds up a septic—this is a level of expertise neither you nor I need to reach. If you rely on a septic system, avoid at all costs (because it can be costly) the use of double-sheeted toilet paper. It really makes for clogs.

■ Much more important than in the city is the need to service heating and cooling equipment. If you are on oil, you should be able to get a yearly check-up as part of your delivery contract. If not oil, talk to your HVAC service person, or to your gas or electric company to see what check-up requirements are necessary for your heating system. Do they have an annual checkup contract? And can they get to your machines without getting into your home?

■ Make sure the air-conditioning service delivers a year's supply of filters with their checkup. It might cost you slightly more than buying the filters on your own, but it is wonderful to have them at the ready.

■ If you plan to be away from your second home for an extended period of time, make the alarm company come out for a checkup before you leave. Push the point. Tell them that you pay them all through the year and it is better to catch any glitch in the system rather than have a dozen false alarms.

■ Talk to the company or the person you have engaged to snowplow your driveway. Go over any concerns you have about plantings or stone edging. If you are really worried, then you or they should put flag markers along the iffy part. They are available at any hardware store.

12

The Great or Not-So Outdoors

> "Oh, give me land, lots of land, under starry skies above, don't fence me in."
>
> Lyrics by Cole Porter, sung by Roy Rogers,
>
> *Don't Fence Me In* (1945)

The ultimately suave Mr. Porter was as ambivalent about this tune as he was about the outdoors.

He was not alone.

For city dwellers venturing into greener pastures, the outdoors holds both charm and chasms. Not the least endangered species will be your city-raised pets.

You are thrilled. Little Violet or Robespierre, after years in the city where outdoors equals a crowded dog park, is going to be treated to wider vistas at your second home.

Wait! Stop right here. Of course you are going to take your pets to the country, the seashore, the mountains. They are part of your family. But especially with dogs, you have to beware what happens when they meet Mother Nature.

My pals Omar and Steve traveled back and forth with many pets between Manhattan and the upper New York countryside. Omar warns:

"The one big thing to remember—for dogs, cats, lizards—is to not let them out in a new place until they're very well adjusted and then do so only with the greatest of care. I've heard of people rushing off, particularly in the spring to a new house, with a cat or dog that's never seen anything but the concrete and soiled patches of snow in Manhattan, and the wild open spaces make them nuts and they run to the first briar patch and refuse to come out or, worse, just keep running. There's no safeguard for this, but animals need time to mark a place and know how to get back. It's better if there's a fenced yard, but this doesn't always help. Also, if they're not fixed, make sure you don't let them out unattended or you may have a passel of lusty hounds leaping over your fence. That happened with our first dog in upstate New York. She snuck away and came back with a very proprietary looking German shepherd about three hours later."

Explore the area around your second home together, with your pet on a leash. And if you have a dog or cat that has never been allowed to roam, don't assume that the country or seashore or mountain is the place to begin. These new territories can be quite overwhelming to an urban pet. Go slow!

What you will want to locate in your second neighborhood is a veterinarian and a pet groomer. There is a national chain of vets, VCA animal hospitals, which, on their Web site, *www.vcapets* .*com*, states that they "operate over 375+ animal hospitals in 37 states across the nation in the VCA network. These hospitals are staffed by over 1600 fully-qualified, dedicated and compassionate veterinarians . . . over 130 are board-certified specialists." These facilities are also sometimes twenty-four-hour emergency vets. I am not advocating a national chain, just suggesting that it is a place to start, especially if you are involved in a VCA hospital near your primary home.

You should have with you your pet's vaccination records—and it wouldn't be bad idea to head to the town hall in your second home community and pay for a dog license. In many small towns, they keep a record of whether dogs and cats live in a house. Then, in time of emergency, the firemen or police know to rescue the animals.

With my spaniels, since I think they are adorable beyond belief and that anyone would aspire to dogsnatch them, I have opted for the preemptive approach to guarantee their rescue. They wear collars with the phone number of the home they are staying in—and instead of their names the collars read, "BIG REWARD." Just put it right out there.

Or you could opt for the microchip, implanted under the dog's skin, with all the relevant information should the pet be lost or stolen. It's a great idea, but I would recommend both approaches, since offering some finder, up front, a sizable reward could bring a more instant response.

I have a glorious groomer, Clips and Dips, nearby. They adhere to my most important dog-grooming rule: The dogs don't have to spend ten hours getting washed, cut, and dried. The groomers there are also very friendly, something I've generally found true of people who take up this profession. One warning: You want to make sure that the smaller operations you might find near second homes have someone on the premises the entire time your dogs are there. If the groomer tells you that she or he steps out for lunch or a break, schedule your pet coiffure during the on-premises hours.

And, coming from the city, you must insure your pet's health by following the anti-flea and tick regimen suggested by the vet—the local vet, that is. Even in very cold weather, in places where ticks and deer and other dangers are rampant, you need to put those monthly doses of Frontline on little Poopsie, even though it smells for a few hours. It is important to you and to your pet.

You must also have an animal evacuation plan. It is not just in major tragedies, such as Katrina, that pets are left behind. If you have traveled to your second home by car, you should already have your laundry basket with leashes, etc., in the car trunk or in your garage. Add to it the following: plastic kitchen trash bags, canned food with pop-tops, and an anti–car sickness prescription from your vet. It doesn't matter that your dog or cat loves riding in the car. What you are looking for is a calm escape in time of emergency, and you want the animal to go to sleep and not be traumatized. Give them a pill!

Gardening and Hands-on Activities with Dirt

People who don't want to get their hands dirty in a city want to return to the land as soon as they acquire a second home. It can be a condo in Palm Springs, an A-frame in the White Mountains, or a spread on the Gulf Coast. No sooner is the mortgage

Omar Hendrix, retired from health administration in New York City and Miami, and his partner, Steve Holloway, the retired Dean of Social Work at Barry University, had houses on Long Island and Ulster County before moving to Florida. They now live in the old-growth section of Fort Lauderdale with many pets. Based on his experiences, these are Omar's hurricane pet evacuation tips.

We had two dogs, two parrots, and a cat for Andrew. It was our first hurricane alert and we ignored it until the day of its arrival and we woke up with the news blasting that we had to leave the beach. In a panic, we packed up the house and then all the animals and drove over the causeway to ride it out in a friend's one-room converted garage. The critters were all well behaved, excepting Piccolo, the green parrot, of course. It's important to leave everyone caged in case there's serious damage and they suddenly sense an escape route. Fortunately, the dogs had a good relationship with the cat and even tried to offer comfort as she pleaded to get out. As you know, animals have a way of anticipating bad weather so they were amazingly subdued yet alert. When the strong winds started up, they grew more restless and needed a lot of stroking, but they remained well behaved even when the grapefruits started blowing around and hitting the sides of the garage.

> "Is your invitation to spread a little fertilizer still open?"
>
> Gregory Peck (to Ava Gardner), *On the Beach* (1959)

in one hand than they want to put a trowel and seeds in the other.

I am a recovering gardener. I was first a gardener in Southern California, where the act of gardening is to throw seeds and plants out the door on Monday and be prepared to cut everything back on Wednesday. I thought I was good at gardening, but I had just picked a place to live where it was impossible to fail.

My relocation to Washington, D.C., taught me many things about showing up in a new neighborhood, ready to garden:

- The best floral things to grow around your second home are the plants and blooming things that your neighbors are already growing. Their yard is solid proof that there are plants that will work at your second home; so if you are on Cape Cod, you grow daylilies and rhododendrons, in New Jersey opt for hydrangeas, in Palm Spring bougainvillea. If your neighbors are not the gardening types, or you feel a compulsion to do them one better, take the advice of a local nursery. And I don't mean the nursery department at the chain hardware store. You need a locally owned nursery, where you can go back for advice and where you can complain when the seventeen low-lying junipers you put in die the first winter.

- Hold back. Don't try to do the entire garden in a single shot. If this is a home that you use only seasonally, you will be anxious for instant gratification. That's why Mother Nature created annuals. Put some big pots of geraniums around. They are unstoppable and, I think, very Italianate. Or petunias or marigolds or whatever strikes your fancy. For satisfaction's sake, if you are planting 300 daffodil bulbs, make sure that they are set to bloom in a month when are you actually using the home.

- Take that first year to see how much of a purist you want to be. I have a vision of thousands of compost holders becoming next year's wheelbarrows or spinning wheels, winding up as planters on the lawns of well-intentioned-but-too-busy second homers.

- Learn about your wildlife neighbors. Deer are voracious eaters and it doesn't do you any good to put in a lovely vegetable garden and have Bambi's friends scarf it up in a single seating. There are lots of good antideer products, including Coyote Urine, which you can buy on the Internet. I have a friend who actually has a dinner party at the beginning of the growing season and asks all her male guests to wee around the perimeter of her garden. I don't know if it's effective, but it certainly is an ice breaker.

- And beware the squirrels. My pal Anne planted hundreds of tulip bulbs and planned to spend the following spring standing beside her picture windows, watching them grow and bloom. Instead she looked on in horror as hordes of squirrels feasted, day after day, on this delicacy.

She attempted many times to go out and chase the squirrels away, but they are determined little critters with a real knack for hunting down bone meal and the tulip bulbs it is nourishing. She now grows daffodils.

- Learn about neighbors' pets. In many older second home communities, it is anathema to put up a fence. Children, dogs, cats, and random people wander over and through your yard. Children can be, in this case, restrained, but a golden retriever who has used your yard for general frolicking purposes under previous ownership is just not going to recognize your property rights.

- If you have neighboring cats that roam, or feral cats, you should be sure to wear gloves while gardening. Toxoplasmosis is carried in cats' feces and the Center for Disease control lists accidentally touching your hands to your mouth after gardening as a primary way of catching this very serious disease.

- No matter how small your outdoor space, if you inhabit your second house during warm weather, give yourself a break and grow some herbs. It costs practically nothing and requires little time. And yet, with some fresh basil, all pastas are authentic; a little thyme goes a long way in a chicken dish; and there is nothing better than Nancy Chudakoff's recipe for Rosemary Popcorn, which she uses as a tasty predinner snack. Heat butter, lemon rind, and rosemary. Pour over popcorn. Grab some of those potted herbs from the supermarket, get a couple of inexpensive planters, and let the sun do its work. Yum!

■ Beware of fence companies! Wow! Talk about markup. If you are opting for a vinyl product—and why wouldn't you—first try a big hardware chain, a Lowe's or Home Depot. You can get the product put in by your local handyman, your contractor, or someone the store refers you to. Check out that price against the fence contractor's. It's worth the time to comparison shop on this one. Also, before ordering any fencing product, check the local codes so you fall within the height limits.

Neglecting my sound advice for moderation, perhaps you want to do this gardening with as much complication and as many pure ingredients as possible. You are not alone. There are, it turns out, more than 13 million *composting* Web sites on the Internet and at least half as many composting accoutrement—bins, systems, all sizes and types of containers that you can put in your backyard and fill with rotting materials. I cannot figure out what deep chord composting strikes in some people, but the cacophony soon rises to symphonic levels and composting becomes a way of life.

My pals Sarah and Victor Kovner commute from Manhattan to Fire Island for eight months of the year—as long as they can stretch spring, summer, and fall. She has a flourishing vegetable and flower garden, surrounded by yards and yards of chicken wire fencing, in her halfhearted attempt to foist off the deer that also commute between Fire Island and the mainland. I secretly believe that Sarah likes the deer coming by for a quick bite. She is so committed to being "green" that she carries her precomposting "material" to her second home, first on the train, and then on the ferry. She also convinces neighbors to bring theirs. This is how Sarah sees her gardening:

The primary thing I take to Fire Island every weekend is the material (vegetable refuse) that I have accumulated during the previous week. I refer to it as "compost," but that will be the result after many weeks in my compost heap there. I save it up in two-quart milk containers in a second refrigerator left in my Manhattan apartment by the previous tenant thirty-five years ago. My garden produces a goodly amount of vegetables, starting in March and continuing through November. When I come back to the city on Sunday (or Monday, later in the season) I bring flowers from my garden, starting with daffodils, then pussy willows, tulips, and all kinds of summer blossoms. They make the trip back on Friday, wilted and ready for the compost heap. Compost, alternatively known as "black gold," will save the world.

Gardening at a second home does not afford the luxury of squeezing in a little planting in an odd hour or two, something manageable in a primary home. This is especially true if you, like most of America, live a hectic life. (Of course you do. That's why you got the second home.)

Susan Spencer, a national correspondent for CBS and for its *48 Hours*, is organized the way only a television reporter can be. She and her husband, the journalist-author Tom Oliphant, have been commuting for more than twenty years between Georgetown in Washington, D.C., and a farm in Rappahannock County, Virginia.

Despite planning, there are snafus. Like the rose-bushes. One year I'd ordered a dozen, replacements for the ones Tom killed when he confused fertilizer with Round-up. I had to have them sent to my office so there would be somebody to receive them. They arrived on a Wednesday. This was fine. The plan was to take them out Friday and plant the little suckers over the weekend. Thursday I learned to my horror that I had to fly off to somewhere Friday for a shoot and be gone for a week. Crisis! So I ended up dashing out to the farm, planting the things literally in the dark with a flashlight, and dashing back—120 miles roundtrip.

The rose garden at Fenway (the name of the Spencer-Oliphant second home) grows in an old cow pen, one used by cows for hundreds of years and thus providing just about the best soil any rose could want. When they first acquired Fenway, Susan weeded the to-be-garden, and then had a neighbor plow it out. And then, she tells this with awe, "I spent months moving large rocks around, making pathways and designs. If someone had told me to come into Georgetown and start hauling rocks, I would have told them they were bonkers. But I love gardening and I love Fenway."

This is *serious* gardening. This is deciding to grow not just the basil, but the tomatoes. There are books and books and books on serious gardening. To figure out if you are a serious gardener, study the account of Steve and Omar, and decide whether you are willing to go through what they did at their country home.

When we were away, it was easy enough to set up sprinkling systems. There are some that aren't all that expensive and work reliably. We also had a lot of potted plants, most of which would be outside in the summer, so they get rain or sprinkled. During the winter months when we went less often, it was easy to force some plants into dormancy and store them in the cellar, or we'd keep them on a sunny, glassed in porch. We would use extra-large drain basins or large aluminum pans to fill up with water, which in the winter would hold them for three weeks or so assuming that the heat was left on fairly low.

(I interrupt Omar to stress the amount of carrying, toting, lugging, watering, caring, potting, and general hard work that constitutes working in a garden for some people.)

In the fall, it took a weekend or two to get the garden put aside for winter—tedious, but the weather is nice then and it's still fun to be out: cutting down perennial branches, checking the fence around the vegetable garden to keep the deer out, mulching. There is game management. We had an infestation of groundhogs for a couple of summers. They can plow down a vegetable garden in one night and then stand up on their hind legs jabbering at you that they're waiting for the next planting. We tried pouring everything down their holes and finally ended up getting some old codger to come over with his shotgun. Deer have to be lived with. I don't think there's a solution—not even bags of musk-ox hair. We did go up and down Broadway one spring, visiting all the beauty parlors to collect hair trimmings which Steve stuffed into pantyhose. It didn't work.

The biggest warning to new-to-the-outdoors gardeners is one involving poison—poison ivy, poison oak, poison sumac. Poison ivy is practically the state plant of Cape Cod—and it is valued for its help in holding on to the sandy cliffs around Cape Cod Bay. You can't dig it up, or you will do harm to the cliff. So, in my constant battle against it touching anyone in my house, I have become familiar with many, many Web sites. One of the best, I believe, is *poisonivy.aesir.com.*

WHAT IS POISON IVY?

Poison ivy is a harmful vine or shrub in the cashew family. It grows plentifully in parts of the United States and southern Canada. Poison ivy usually grows as a vine twining on tree trunks or straggling over the ground. But the plant often forms upright bushes if it has no support to climb upon. Species related to poison ivy include poison oak, which grows in the Pacific Northwest and nearby regions of Canada, and poison sumac, which grows in the eastern United States. Poison oak and poison sumac both are shrubs. The tissues of all these plants contain poisonous oil somewhat like carbolic acid. This oil is extremely irritating to the skin. It may be brushed onto the clothing or skin of people coming in contact with the plants. Many people have been poisoned merely by taking off their shoes after walking through poison ivy. People can get poisoned from other people, but only if the oil remains on their skin. The eruptions themselves are not a source of infection. Appearance: The leaves of poison ivy are red in early spring. Later in spring, they change to shiny green. They turn yellow, red, or orange in autumn. Each leaf is made up of three leaflets more or less notched at the edges. Two of the leaflets form a pair on opposite sides of the leafstalk, while the third stands by itself at the tip of the leafstalk. Small greenish flowers grow in bunches attached to the main stem close to where each leaf joins it. Later in the season, clusters of poisonous, berrylike drupes form. They are whitish, with a waxy look.

Control and treatment: Efforts have been made to destroy these plants by uprooting them or by spraying them with chemicals. But poison ivy and poison oak are so common that such methods have not been very effective in eliminating them. Contact with the plants should be avoided. After the oil has touched the skin, it usually takes some time for it to penetrate and do its damage. Before this happens, it is wise to wash the skin thoroughly several times with plenty of soap and water. Care should be taken not to touch any part of the body, for even tiny amounts of the oil will cause irritation. If poisoning develops, the blisters and red, itching skin may be treated with dressings of calamine lotion, Epsom salts, or bicarbonate of soda. Scientists have developed a vaccine that can be injected or swallowed. But this is effective only if taken before exposure.

Remember the primary warning: "Leaves of three, let it be."

Water Everywhere

Second homes frequently have one thing in common—water.

Fresh or salt, flowing or frozen, it's water, water everywhere.

You are faced with two dilemmas: what to put in the water, what to keep out of it. It seems absurd, but the presence of water—natural and pure and perhaps even bubbly as in the ads on TV—is a destructive, nasty menace. Nothing can mess up your floors or upholstered furniture faster than water. Nothing stays around to do more damage. And nothing provides more hazards to you and your guests.

And if it's not bad enough, people frequently increase their water access by building a pool! This is an area ripe for control.

The iron rule at the pool: *Nothing breakable is allowed—ever.* You will be surprised how many adult men and women refuse to understand this rule, how many will wander out of the French doors, carrying a porcelain coffee cup, to *ooh* and *ah* over the sunrise. Stop them in their tracks. Be firm. One broken cup or glass will haunt you for months.

Plastic or paper must be the only containers allowed. Target has really attractive semi-permanent plastic stuff, cheap enough so that at the end of a year, you can toss it. But you probably can't put it in the dishwasher. So use the heavy-duty plastic trays or bowls for salad or chips, and paper for plates and cups.

I opt for throwaways. You use them and they disappear. I know they are not environmentally ideal, but I am using and washing cotton napkins so I get a break. Also, urge guests to drink their sodas and beers right out of the cans at poolside. The cheapie stores have those old-fashioned basket-weave paper plate holders. Don't turn up your nose. They allow you to use inexpensive paper plates without having people's frankfurters dive into the pool.

And what else goes in the pool?

Pretty much anything people leave poolside.

Having lost one cell phone (it sizzled when it hit the chlorinated water) and the nice watch of a guest (squished when he moved his deck chair), I have a new approach. I have invested in a dozen small plastic boxes, the kind sold in cute colors at the Container Store, the ones undergraduates buy for dorm rooms but never utilize.

When we have a crowd, I spread the boxes out on a table on the pool patio. I ask people to take one, stick their stuff in it, and understand that unless they put the box back on the table, its contents have good chance of being waterlogged by the end of the day.

And what else goes in the pool?

In my world, only children with life vests or expensive floaties or waterwings are permitted in the water. That little plastic duckie thing around a three-year-old's waist won't do her a bit of good if her brother trips her into the pool. And the parent must be with any child under the age of seven—hands on, with the kid, in the pool.

And what else goes in the pool?

Babies do wee in the pool, no matter what the mother says, and so I insist on waterproof diapers. No one, not even family members, wants to splash around in baby wee, so that's that.

And what else goes in the pool?

No food. Not on rafts, or being eaten while the swimmer hangs onto the side. You want to really clog up a filtration system, try dropping some jalapeño poppers into the water.

What is at poolside is just as important. And please note—everything that follows is just as crucial at homes at the side of a lake, a pond, a canal, a river.

Keep a first-aid kit handy. (Not the same as the one you keep in the house.) Again, use one of those Container Store boxes, this one with a top and handles. Put in a good selection of Band-Aids, some antibiotic ointment, a couple of big patches, tweezers, some matches, a bottle of water, an anti-itch pencil, calamine lotion. Keep a large supply of sun-screen and lotion on hand, in a yet bigger plastic box.

And put both of those plastic boxes in a plastic trunk that you put near the pool—or on the dock or stick the box on a wagon so it can get pulled to the beach. (There is a wide range of costs in plastic storage trunks, enough so that a comparison of brands is worthwhile. Rubbermaid and Suncrest are two of the most available.) Have a second large container with "outside" towels. These can be as threadbare or campy as you desire. Do not let people use your lovely white bath towels outside. Do not under any circumstances let family or guests take these towels to the beach or the pool. Keep indoor and outdoor towels segregated—and if you think that's being Miss Fussy-pants, think about the rank dampness of a pool towel, the sandiness of a beach towel, or better yet, a towel that has spent several days in the bottom of a boat.

And Then It Freezes . . .

In cold weather second homes, water is just as insidious.

Snow turns to water; snow turns to sludge then turns to dirty water.

However you work it out, in a cold climate, you must have a "mud room." Doesn't that just say it all! Keep that nasty, wet, damp stuff outside of the main part of the house—even if the house is a condo.

This requires cleverness and planning. The smallest ski chalet probably has a teeny powder room near the front door. You can make this your *mudette-toilette*. Put large, sturdy hooks on the wall—big ones—and anchor them in. Tell people that's where to hang their anoraks and ski jackets. Ask guests to leave clean and dry socks in a basket outside the door of the powder room—or buy a couple dozen pair of white athletic socks and be a real sport. When they take off their jackets and boots, have guests drop their wet socks into a second basket and run the socks through the washer-dryer at the end of the day. If their T-shirts or jeans are soaked, throw them in along with the socks.

It's worth it. Nothing smells worse than a wet dog unless it is a wet sock, draped over a heater somewhere. Wool hats, mufflers, and gloves are the bane of cold-weather existence. They come with a built-in wet-dog smell, which a drop of snow instantly releases.

And if you have dogs along in the snow or the sleet or the rain—be nice to them and get them a jacket. L. L. Bean has very attractive, water-resistant plaid doggie blankets that have Velcro to hold them in place and the dog's name can be monogrammed on free of charge. Even if you have a galloping, snow-loving dog, the blanket-coat will keep the dog from getting totally soaked. Also handy are the micro-fiber dog-drying gloves, available in most pet stores. Any dog that has been to the groomers should and can be dried off with a hand-held hair dryer. Even a few minutes with the dryer will make a huge difference in the amount of moisture on the dog and in your house.

If you are in a country house, in a place where snow comes and goes but mud stays, you are just going to have to accommodate your dog bringing a lot of dirt into the house. You can train the dog to stay in the mudroom until he dries off, or in the kitchen if you have a washable floor. You can brush the dog off several times a day. Or you can just say, "This is country life," and get on with baking bread.

13

Entertaining

> "You must come again . . . You promised to have a family dinner with us. I've not forgot, you see. At least three courses."
>
> Mrs. Bennett, *Pride and Prejudice* (timeless)

Friends and Flambés

The quickest way to end a long-standing friendship is during the short sitting of a dinner party. You know that. Two persons, who you absolutely adore but don't know each other well, argue during the antipasto, explode during the entree, and pout during the pie. We've had it happen or seen it enough times in film and on TV to experience the comic aftermaths or the tragic consequences.

There are a lot of questionable scenarios when you mix primary home friends and second home friends. You never thought about that? You never thought that the accountant who works in the next office, who you share lunch with a couple times a week, wouldn't be able to abide the cowboy who is your neighbor in Montana? How about the Chicago lawyer who you find a little too liberal—put him beside the retired merchant mariner who is your fishing buddy in Sanibel? Or your friend from your children's nursery school days who knows that some people live together without benefit of clergy, but who certainly hasn't met any of them. That's right—just invite her right up to Sun Valley.

Of course there are differences, except in Manhattan, where exactly the same people see each other both at the primary and second homes. Mostly we have different friends in our second home location. You might have an old college friend nearby, or a sister or a brother who loves your second home location as much as you do. But, unless you plan to import your entire social life, you have to become part of your neighborhood. Here are some simple approaches to try:

- Track down anyone you know, either in your second home town or nearby—could be a school friend, somebody who moved from your primary residence home town, or even a friend of a friend. Reach out. Don't be concerned if you don't love this person. You are not marrying them. You are going to make a plan to play golf or have lunch or dinner or simply a drink. You don't know who you might meet through them. It's the launch of your new life.
- Reach out to your neighbors by reaching out. Have a neighborhood party sometime during your first season in your house. It doesn't have to be fancy—a picnic will

do, or "sips and snacks." You'll have to ascertain if en-tertaining in your new second home area requires a full-stacked bar. Try to talk to every single person there at least once.

- You bought your house here because you love this place, its ambience, the speed (whether waltz or warp). Okay. Now learn the rules that govern it. Don't, for example, try to have a disco night in a neighborhood where even Brahms is considered raucous.

- Join something. Anything. A book club, a gardening club, a ski club, a water safety club—anything that makes you a part of the neighborhood. Subscribe to the neigh-borhood newspaper. Go to neighborhood meetings or town meetings or city council meetings. Certainly you should be there, if only to protect your investment in the neighborhood.

- Chat people up! People in the community pool, at the hairdressers, after church. You think I am being too pushy about this, and you are afraid of being pushy. Be-lieve me, in a second home community, almost everyone was once a stranger or they are too old to know the dif-ference. And they are all looking for new blood!

So once you've made friends in your second home neighbor-hood and have people you can walk with, ski with, lunch with, share books with, you've got to figure out how to shuffle them and your hometown friends together. Or do you?

Maybe some groups are better left unshuffled. It's like mixing friends from a first and second marriage—at some point you are asking yourself, Who are these people and why have I brought them all together?

That doesn't mean that you can't have a gargantuan New Year's Eve or a fabulous Fourth with all elements: dancing, singing, drinking, eating. But the reason those kind of events work with a mixture of friends is that there are so many festivities that you can't get trapped in the after dinner conversation or the *après ski* cocktail.

This becomes slightly more complicated when your second home is in the proximity of other second homes and there is a lot of visiting and socializing back and forth. I've found the best way to deal with this is to be completely honest—up to a point!

If you are having a friend, a couple, a group from another piece of your life come to visit and you want time alone with them, be sure to give your second home neighborhood pals a heads-up. Tell them that you're out of the local social swing for a weekend or even a week. Let them know that your usual availability is on hiatus. This is especially true if you live in a community where people "drop by." Now there is a concept I can do without, especially when the dropper opens the door and, after a quick identifying shout, strolls right in. If someone wants to visit me, they can use that unique instrument of connection, the telephone, and ring me up and tell me they're going to "drop by." (I know of a quick cure if you are not the drop-by-able type and you have a neighbor who doesn't get the message: the next time he or she is headed up your garden path, strip to your undies, and greet them at the door with an oh-my-gosh-you-should've-phoned-first. It's a winner!)

You can decide to mix your two sets of friends, either at a

cocktail party, or take a risk and have a sit-down dinner. But I would go slowly down this road. You are putting down roots in this second home community. And friends who come to visit are frequently friskier on vacation than they would be at home—or if this were *their* second home, truth be told. The potential for strife and drama is great!

One final caution: Establish early on what the rules are about houseguests being other people's guests. Every community has its own standard on whether it is proper and appropriate to bring along your guests when you are invited to special gatherings. There are fine lines. Yes, it's okay or even swell for a cocktail party or a brunch, but what about a dinner party? And what about a celebratory event, like an anniversary party or a birthday party? These are situations that must be negotiated with great care, or your social canoe will be swamped.

My advice is to always, I mean always, check with the person or people giving the party. Don't let a casual "come on down" at the market or the third tee be sufficient reason for you to drag four extra people along to a shindig in honor of someone they have never heard of.

If the host seems a little squeamish, you can either bring your guests for a short drop by, which equals one drink and two canapés, and doesn't include dinner. Or, if it is something you really want to go to, make a plan for your houseguests that night that does not include you—like sending them to dinner at your expense at a local bistro or having cooked lobsters delivered.

Again, good manners must prevail, despite the social mores that claim that "your guests and my guests are our guests."

"I like to have a martini,

Two at the very most.

After three I'm under the table,

After four I'm under my host!"

Attributed to Dorothy Parker

Hosting Events

I classify events into three categories: big, really big, and so large that you wish you had never gotten into this in the first place.

The relative size of any celebratory event is logically calibrated on what you have to offer—if you are in a town house, even one with a community party room, there will be stringent limitations, while on a farm you can fill the pastures. But beware, whatever the size of your layout, guest lists can grow to fill the available space. A second warning—a wedding, or any large event, will take its toll not just for the day of the party, but for a week before and a week after. Take this into consideration before announcing, "we'd love to do it."

No matter the prewedding jitters, the ceremony, reception, or some part of the event is frequently held in a second home. If you have any sort of a view and even the shabbiest of yards, it will be prettier by far than the nearest chapel, chateau, or caterer. And it will be cheaper—an even more important consideration in weddings these days, as the "destination wedding" has thrown the price of nuptials totally out of kilter.

If you are allowing your second home to be part of an event, *and the event is not featuring an immediate member of the family*, you should establish some ground rules from the get-go:

- If your home is being used for the ceremony—wedding or party of any sort—then no guests should be staying at your home. This should be a firm rule, unless you have hot-and-cold running household staff and a slew of bedrooms. You don't need people pushing the caterer out of the way in search of the morning coffee and you will need your home to yourself the day after the event to regroup.
- Set a size on the event on day one. Any caterer or tent supplier or party rental operation will be able to tell you how many feet are required for each table and chairs. A rule of thumb is that you need the diameter of the table and then at least 2 feet on each side of or around the table for seating. Many people want more space. You cannot do with less. Make it clear that you know how many people fill your space—and be firm.
- Make sure that the people throwing the event know what is available hotel-motel-B&B-wise. If it's a large group and your second home is near Lenox, Massachusetts, they cannot schedule an event during the summer when the music festival at Tanglewood is in full swing. Ditto Ashland, Oregon, with Shakespeare going on. Or Anywhere, U.S.A., on the Fourth of July. It's their responsibility to book the rooms or arrange the sleeping arrangements. It's your responsibility to tell them what's on their agenda.
- If a caterer is being used, you want an early-on meeting with the catering supervisor. Are they bringing in their

own kitchen in a truck with a portable setup to function outside, or are they planning to use yours? I would advise keeping that caterer in that little truck as much as possible. And I would stress that your utensils, plates, dishes, glasses, and linen are simply off-limits. It is much easier for the caterer to bring in clean and take out dirty; most caterers prefer it that way. If everyone is coming from another place, you will probably have to scare up recommendations for caterers, too. Do not trust anything that is served up at a "tasting." Lucille, my cocker spaniel, could probably cook two pieces of veal perfectly and make a lovely "tasting." Scout out caterers by going to someone else's event and seeing how the food looks and tastes when it is served up in large proportions.

■ Flowers and music are not your problem. Unless you have offered to "give" this wedding, stay away from these details. For an at-home event, I would advise keeping these elements as simple as possible. If there is going to be dancing, insist that some kind of a portable dance floor be brought in by the rental people.

■ If you live in a condo community and are planning to use the "party room," check out its availability before making any promises. And check out if the facility is being used either the day before or after the event. It would be a smart-cookie thing to do if you booked the room for all three days. Usually the room's cost involves a nominal cleanup fee, but it would insure that your bride and groom weren't playing pin-the-tail with the neighbor's birthday grandchild.

■ *Safety!* If you have a pool, if you are on a lake or a river or a stream or the ocean, you must have a trained EMT on hand for a large event. No ifs, ands, or buts. And it's especially true if you are having children as guests. Let's face it: If you are having an event with dozens of people at your home, most of whom you don't know, you should be sure to have a person who knows about emergency situations. And the bride or groom or birthday person or anniversary couple who asked you to use your house should pay for that EMT. You can't go back and redo an emergency. No, it doesn't help that Cousin Rita is a registered nurse or that Uncle Peter is a doctor. You need an emergency professional and one who is from your second home neighborhood. It's the sensible way to go.

■ A celebration will probably include the consumption of alcohol. You have to set more ground rules. That could include whether or not underage drinkers will be allowed a glass of champagne or even access to the bar; will someone be keeping an eye on tipsy guests, making sure that they don't get behind a wheel (in many states, you, the homeowner, could be responsible for whatever havoc they cause); will there be a time when the bar is turned off; and a firm time for the festivities to end.

Now, getting down to the gritty of giving an event where *you* are the party planner. My first step would be to get help. So, you want to have fifty people for a daughter's wedding, a spouse's significant birthday, or to celebrate you. (What a great idea!) Doing it yourself doesn't mean that other people can't help (although to trust a big-time celebration to potluck dishes is madness). Take control! If it's the old "loving hands at home" approach, it has to be organized beyond a professional party planner's wildest dreams.

- Follow Santa's dictum: Make a list, check it twice. Getting a solid guest list together is the first priority. Everything else is going to depend on how many people are coming. If your second home is quite a trek for some of the potential invitees, it is perfectly polite to ring them up and ask them about their availability.

- If the event will require people staying overnight in nearby B&Bs or motels, check the availability of these accommodations on your proposed date. This is now your responsibility as the party giver, and when you are checking, do figure out if you can get a group rate at one of the larger establishments. They will set up an account with your party name on it and guests can simply phone in, make their reservations, get their discounts, and pay their bills. If it is a practice in your neighborhood to farm out guests if you are hosting a big event, do so with great diplomacy. Older guests need a real bedroom and probably a private bath. Guests with kids needs some real guidance. And, of course, anyone you are using as a makeshift B&B host should both be invited to the big event and sent a warm thank-you afterward, along with a bottle of wine or a pretty plant.

- If you are planning the event months in advance, try to plan your garden or the patio pots to flower at the appropriate time. If you are doing this fete in the winter months in a cold and somewhat isolated place (read ski area or northern country), try to avoid flowers, unless it is around Christmas and you can scoop up poinsettias in the local supermarket. You can easily spray twigs and branches silver and white and pop them into cheap red vases. You can fill glass bowls with pinecones, again sprayed gold or silver. You can buy inexpensive round, frameless mirrors and edge them with votive candles.

■ Whatever you do, try to get the cheapest tables and chairs. Some communities have a center or a club or a "party room," and they also make available to their members/constituents folding chairs and tables. Perhaps your church would loan you some, or you can check with the Elks or the VFW to see if they rent out their spares. If you are planning on doing a lot of entertaining for a lot of people over the next few years, check with the party rental people. They are usually in some stage of upgrading and you don't care how scarred the tabletop may be. Buy several "rounds" and stick them in the basement or garage.

■ If you've managed to score some cheapo or free seating, a quick and economical way to do tablecloths is using sheets; try king-size sheets, tucked under and pinned, in a kind of harem-skirt manner. If you want to get fancy, buy secondhand tablecloths at the flea market, and drape them over the tabletops, a square or a rectangle over the round table.

■ If you are using long tables, either rentals or folding tables bought or borrowed, the best covers are the ones that don't get tangled around the guests' legs. On the top of each table, put an old mattress cover and cut it so it hangs over the table edge about four inches. Then take whatever tablecloth you've come up with and your staple gun, and staple both the pad and the tablecloth to the underside of the folding table. *Voilà!* A great look although not always permanent. (Cheapo plastics are funky but interesting, especially if you can get them in somewhat attractive colors, or use your old tablecloths, the ever popular sheet or, again, check the jobbers.)

- For dishes, follow the real-estate maxim: Don't rent if you can buy! Go to any discount-jobber-outlet store. Look for cheap dishes (we're talking $1 a piece). White is best because all white dishes blend together, no matter the shape or size. Buy twice as many as you will need— that's right, twice. You are going to serve your dinner on a full-size plate and do the same with your dessert. I urge anyone undertaking an "event" and doing the cooking themselves to go big on desserts. Try serving several and put them all on the same plate. Mix 'n match chocolate cake, cheesecake, cookies, and a fruit salad. It seems elaborate and extravagant and it's easy.

- Glassware for at-home events done by you is always a question. Nobody wants to do the wineglasses for fifty people, especially when you know that glasses will be left half full and new ones will be on demand at the bar. This is a decision only you can make, because only you know how "proper" you are. Plastic is plastic and it just isn't very nice, so if you are having four dozen people to a family wedding, go out and buy cheap wineglasses. IKEA is a great source—about half the cost of renting—but don't start speaking Bob's Nordic tongue.

■ Hire serving and cleanup help—or you will be the servant at your own party. You are an expert cook and a great host/hostess. That doesn't mean you have to be the one to scrape the lasagna out of the bottom of the pans. Seriously, you have saved a fortune by doing the party yourself. Don't think you have to also be the scullery maid.

■ You may want to opt for "heavy hors d'oeuvres" and a deluge of desserts. First, the canapés. Near the beach: shrimp and small crab cakes and, please, either buy fresh or have your local seafood place whip them up. Nothing goes faster than pigs in a blanket. Teeny hamburgers are all the rage at fancy parties. It is worth the time and a small investment in the weeks before your party to experiment with the frozen appetizers from your supermarket or, better, from BJ's or Costco. Whatever you serve, make sure if you are serving alcoholic beverages that you give people enough to eat. An appetizer-only party should be one where the treats just keep on coming.

Many if not all of these points apply at a primary home. But it is at a second home that you will have to make decisions as to whether to rent or to scrounge, whether you can find help for a party, and in almost every case, what to do about parking.

If your second home is in the country and you just plan to

have people pull their cars up on your front lawn: Warn them. Millions of faille and patent shoes have died an early death due to smothering by sod. If your guests are coming from nearby homes, they might know how rugged parking is, but even then, advise people to bring "sensible shoes" to get into the house.

If you are in a town house or condo or in an older single-residence community where streets are narrow and parking spaces are meager, you probably have to arrange for shuttle parking. Check in with your municipality and see if a publicly owned parking lot is available, either for rent or merely by request. You need to make this arrangement months in advance of the event, especially if most guests will be arriving by car and you want to include the parking instructions in the invitation. Then you need to rent a shuttle. Or you need to mobilize many friends with vans.

If your event is a simple one—that's the term we use when we try to deny that a dinner, cocktail party, luncheon or drop-by will involve as much work as we know it will—then there are still some rules that will keep it under control.

- For cocktail parties, serve only room temperature or cold "snacks." If you must have Pigs in a Blanket, buy the box of prepared piggies at BJ's. No one is expecting gourmet at a second home—and if they are, they can do it at their house.
- An exception would be fundraisers. So often in a second-home area, community wide events get organized around raising money for a local arts center, a day camp—or, yes, a candidate. And you have succumbed to lending your house for the event. Sorry, but you have

to pony up and serve some pricy or at least complicated food when people write a check to attend.

■ You can always get away with being "cute." My son Michael had an annual St. Patrick's Day party for sixty-plus and served only beer and Lucky Charms cereal, with the shamrocks. My friend Diane and I gave the pre-party dinner for a weekend celebrating our pal Linda's 60th—and themed the appetizers to her "decades," with cheese spread and Ritz crackers for the 1940s, onion dip for the '50s, Pigs for the '60s. You get the idea.

Kathleen Hendrix, a writer, journalist and world traveler who works evaluating non-profit organizations, is a great friend and amazing cook who now lives part of the year in Canandaigua, New York. She calls this recipe Borneo Beans, since that is where she learned to cook them when she was in the Peace Corps. "I sometimes try something else, when I am cooking for a special occasion with friends, but these are the ones people always ask for."

Green Beans, about 2 pounds

Onions, one or two sliced into thin crescents

Vegetable oil (not olive)

Salt

Dried Cayenne pepper flakes

Continued on next page

(continued from previous page)

Snap ends off beans and wash; rinse in colander; leave kind of wet; set aside. Heat oil in large skillet; when hot, put in onions and cook, stirring until at least at the soft stage. Dump the beans in, salt liberally and shake pepper flakes in to taste; cover for a few minutes, keeping heat fairly high. This steams the beans, hastening the cooking. Uncover when water dries up, stir the beans and onions while you continue to burn the daylights out of them. My discerning guests like them when they see a few blackened onion slices and green beans among them. Sea salt is especially good for this. If you disapprove of salt, I suggest forgetting this recipe and steaming some green beans in the microwave.

14

Acquiring Your (Almost) Dreamhouse

> "It's lavish, but I call it home."
>
> Clifton Webb, *Laura* (1944)

Turning a Rental into Your Very Own Second Home

My neighbor, Baroness Mary Goudie, knows a lot about houses, perhaps because she is a member of the British House of Lords. She spends a chunk of every summer on Cape Cod. Although she and her husband, James, are now proud home-owners, they rented for their first several years. It was probably all that historic UK experience of showing up in strange countries and making them very British, but Mary indeed had the knack of turning a drab but well-situated cottage into her own castle in a single day.

If you are going to live in a rental for more than a week, it is worth the time on the very first day to make the home or condo truly comfortable for you. If you are returning to a home that you have rented before, you know what it's missing—nice wineglasses, good pillows, and an arrangement of furniture in the living room that allows people to talk to each other after dinner. If it's your first time in a rental, try to scope out what would make it more your own; it could be some throws or a set of your old dishes or even your good coffee pot. (No one over the age of eight has to eat dinner off plastic dishes, especially ones with blue Pennsylvania Dutch hex signs.) This is harder if you are flying to your rental, but that is why UPS and FedEx exist.

Watching Mary make the rental her very own gave me some tips that anyone could follow to perform a similar feat:

- Don't be afraid of moving furniture. Mary had a swell enclosed seaside porch, about eight feet wide, with a tile floor. She traded the few uncomfortable plastic casual chairs for the dining table and chairs and, *voilà,* had a breathtaking dining room overlooking the sea.
- She bought a set of dishes and a set of inexpensive wineglasses and simply left the tacky rental stuff in the cabinet. After the first year, she installed her own bed clothes in the master and had a pleasant set of towels. (All of these "added touches" lived in my basement and attic during the winter.)
- She sent all personal decorative items left by the owners to an upstairs closet, and put snapshots of her summer friends around the living room, along with a pretty platter and some decorative coasters on the coffee table. It doesn't take a lot—just out with theirs and in with yours.

■ She ignored the obligatory and half-consumed staples that the owners insisted on leaving in what should have been her kitchen cabinets and simply commandeered a counter for her own cereal, sugar, etc. (I would have simply tossed the junk the owners left, but I am not such a polite person and Mary wanted to continue to rent the house until she bought her own.)

■ The most important thing the Baroness did was decide that she was in a lovely place and not let the inadequacy of the rental house mar her holiday. "Stiff upper lip" and "White Cliffs of Dover" and all that. It is easier said than done.

You, a renter, could wind up in a real rats' nest—bad beds, tattered sheets, little critters sharing the house—a situation not fixed by a couple of Votivo candles and a few chenille throws. If so, you have some, although limited, recourses.

If you have rented through a local agency, get them on the phone immediately. Agents are usually licensed and don't want a problem. If it is a matter of how the house was cleaned previous to your arrival, make them send someone over. If it is the general condition of the furniture, sheets, etc., you've got a harder fight. You could tell the agent that you want an allowance to go out and get decent sheets, pillows, whatever. I'm not sure what that gets you, but it is worth a try.

While you are at it, don't be afraid to demand a better house. Agents usually are leasing several homes in the area during the season, which is especially true with condos in a ski area. Although the owners of the unit you were first given will be very angry about losing your rental fee, there is no question that the leasing agent will be upset that the owners left the house in such disastrous condition.

If you have rented off the Internet—many agents as well as individuals rent that way today—you could demand some kind of assistance, again cleaning or household items. And you could also say that you plan to post a very disagreeable letter on their Web site or with the managers of the Web site, saying how they misrepresented the house they rented to you.

Some nastiness at a rented second home can be removed with a small outlay of cash. If the pillows are sticky, but the view is sublime, go to the nearest discount store and buy some pillows. Ditto with the sheets and towels. If the chairs are totally uncomfortable, run to the nearest supermarket or hardware store and get a couple of plastic ones. I know. You've paid a lot of money to rent this place and it is not up to your or any decent renter's expectations. But if you only have a short time, and the mountain trails are calling and the fish are jumping in the lake, go enjoy and make the best of it. And please, do not leave any of your purchased additions behind. Even if you have to dump them in the nearest Goodwill box, at least have the satisfaction of not leaving the house better than the way you found it.

Buying a Second Home

My first suggestion in buying a second home: Look for a house in a place you really love—and that will love you back.

If that seems obvious, let me assure you that the road to

second homes is littered with dashed dreams, crammed with folks who are golfers but bought hours from a course, or sailors with a house many miles from open water, or even folks who hate to drive with a second home in a place accessible only by auto.

Your search needs to begin with some structural soul searching. What do you need and want in a second home: Is a scenic view something special to you? Do warm or cold or middling temperatures turn you on? Do you want a small community— new construction or old? Do you want a certain level of services, like trash collection and a professional, paid fire department? Are there substantial medical services nearby? Do you have a cat, dog, or horse that has to be accommodated? Is it a neighborhood friendly to children and are children's activities available nearby?

Again, the obvious isn't always so. If you are looking for a house with a view, especially a view of the water, be it ocean, bay, pond, or lake, you need to do the search in the late spring or summer. I am sure you have heard about the propensity of trees to sprout leaves. Leaves, when grouped together with trees, have a forest effect that blocks the view. At the Cape, a house that has its view blocked for six months of the year is called a "winter view" house. That says it all, especially if you plan to use such a house only in warm weather.

Views are the ultimate endangered species. If you are in the country and want to ensure a pastoral scene, your only true option is to ante up and buy the surrounding acreage. Don't let the Realtor assure you that the old-timer next door is never going to build on those two lots that abut your potential property. In resort areas, in prime country spaces (with the exception of

Montana, where you never have to see anyone), on the beaches and lakes and mountains, just believe that everything eventually gets built up.

The temperature thing is vital. I don't know how many people have told me they were thinking of getting a place in either North Carolina or in Oregon who then couldn't tell me how hot or cold it was in those climes. Northern New York is cold. So is Michigan. Idaho can be hot or cold or perfect, as the people who have homes in Sun Valley tell me. Sante Fe is a dozen-plus degrees colder than nearby Alburquerque in the winter. Northern California is cold or chilly or not very hot. Look, if you are an outdoors type and want to hike or swim or ski or snowboard or anything to do with being outside, if the place isn't obviously snowbound or sun-drenched, really check out the monthly temperatures, which can be easily found on the Internet.

So now you've narrowed down your search to a specific area, several towns or communities, and you are somewhat familiar with them. If you've summered or wintered there, spent time as a guest, have great pals who live nearby, half your work is done. But, as the classic Jacqueline Susann epic is titled: "Once is not enough." And somewhat is not sufficient. Go to the prospective community and spend some cash for a long weekend or even a week in a comfortable motel-hotel. Drive around. Go to the super-markets. Stop by the golf club and inquire about membership. Eat in a variety of restaurants. How late are they open? Are they open in the off-season? If you attend religious services regularly, check out the places of worship. Are there year-round services? Are people friendly in the local stores? Is there a big-box store or a mega-supermarket within an easy drive? If you are a boater, are there slips available? Whoops—now that was almost a slip. You just found out that there is a four-year wait for a mooring at the local marina!

If your second home requires a somewhat lengthy or complicated commute, take the actual journey both ways. Don't rely on what friends who live there tell you. If you are planning to commute by plane or train or bus or ferry or car on a regular basis, then make sure you try your planned method out before you buy. If you are going from Richmond to Sanibel for a month each winter, and you are going to travel by car train, then take the train, at least one way. If you are commuting between Philadelphia and Mackinaw Island, and "everyone" has told you that the drive is a piece of cake, try it out. If you are heading from San Diego to Beaver Creek, make sure there is more than one airline servicing that route. And that the schedule doesn't radically change from winter to summer.

Despite being a dispenser of good advice, I haven't always followed it. In the small community which is now home to my primary home, I bought my first house after my husband and I had a one-night stay with old friends, George and Barbara Thibault. We had arrived after dark, but the next morning, with the sun bouncing off Cape Cod Bay, I announced that Bob and I should live right there, forever. George jokingly sent me to his next-door neighbor, the local real estate maven, Barbara Sullivan. I told her that, having sold our second home in New Jersey, I was in the market for a new second home. Now! I wanted a house right now! And one on the beach, please!

Standing in her doorway in her robe (it was early), she smiled and said that nothing, simply nothing was for sale in this established neighborhood of summer homes to many generations of a few families. I told her that was all right, but as soon as something came for sale, with any kind of a view, we'd buy it.

And we did, several months later. But not on the water, which is what I craved. Especially one old pile a couple of blocks down the beach that I fixated on, and was told would never be for sale. Several months later, when it was and when I was convinced that I could sell our first purchase quickly, we bought it—before we ever saw the inside.

It was pleasantly horrific, the perfect second home from the 1950s, virtually untouched, with shag carpeting and the best views from the second floor blocked by huge closets in the corners of the house. It was a construction battle from day one— permits, plans, permissions, possibilities—but it is indeed the house of our dreams.

Wait! It might not turn out so well for you. Only buy emotionally if you can handle the emotional ups and downs. That means that if you so want a house, a place, a view, a feeling—yes, a feeling—that you are willing to put up with finding raccoons in the bathroom, a foundation that doesn't meet up with the house, five decades of misuse, and a lot of head-shaking by family and friends who think you've gone over the edge, then just go ahead and buy the thing.

More later on emotions, but first, how should you proceed when buying a second home?

You've chosen a location, and then you have to choose a Realtor. My advice is to interview three and pick one. And stick with that one. You're smart and you'll get a feeling for someone you want to work with. There are only a few places that still don't subscribe to the multiple-listings phenomenon. In most places, every Realtor can get you into every house.

One caveat: In some smaller communities, some of the best properties never go on the market. The connected Realtor has a list of "prospective buyers," and this special list of subscribers gets called before the For Sale sign gets pounded into the front lawn. If you are looking in a community where homes rarely come on the market or if you have a special list of requirements, then you need to look for a Realtor who has a special relationship to that community. In most resort or second-home condominiums, one Realtor prevails, and you will figure that out by reading the real-estate listings or by talking to the doorman or manager in a building you are interested in or the folks who run the local businesses.

Some of my best friends are Realtors. That doesn't mean that other Realtors don't play a somewhat cagey game. They all want to sell their own listings first. Why not, since it means that they get the entire 5 percent (the usual) fee. Some will even be so protective of their fee that they will only show you their listings. Up front, at the beginning, say you want to see *everything* that is anywhere near your price range. Tell the Realtor not to be limited by what you say would be perfect; you want to look at the four-and-five bedroom as well as the two-bedroom homes. Ask, before you sign on with a Realtor, if you can look at the actual Multiple Listing Service printout—and I mean the whole pile, not just what they pick out for you.

Getting a big picture of the market will be good for you, as a buyer, since you will get an even greater grasp of how strong the overall market is in this second home community. Ask the Realtor, who knows more about properties than the MLS tells you, just how long a specific house has been on the market. Then ask whether the property was on the market, pulled off, and then put back on—so that it looks fresh, listed as having been up for sale for a couple of weeks instead of many months. Find out if any property you are interested in has had a previous offer on it, and if so, ask why the offer was withdrawn. Most states insist that Realtors tell the truth on the matter of previous offers, but lips seem to button up when a Realtor is asked why the offer was withdrawn.

When you find your potential dream house, have a little visit. Stay for an hour or so. That's right. Make the Realtor just stay right there with you as you roam around the house and really check out what you like or dislike about it.

I am not implying that you do a house inspection.

No. I want you to do a heart-and-soul inspection. This is supposed to be your sanctuary, your refuge, your place for getting away, whether alone or with a cast of hundreds. See how this potential purchase *feels* to you. Don't worry about cabinets or closets. Is there a nice flow between the kitchen and the rest of the house? Are the bedrooms piled one on top of each other, or could you have some privacy? Is the yard big enough or small enough for your desires? Is the view—or lack of it—a deal breaker?

Sit in various rooms. Sit on the chairs, on the beds, on the tub, on a kitchen stool. Look around. Do you see yourself in this house? Can this place, with as little or as much work as you want to do, be made into someplace you will love coming to stay?

Almost any problem with any house can be fixed by throwing money at it. Walls can be moved, additions can be built, kitchens can be redesigned. But you can't fix the major temperament of a house. Imagine your furniture, or at least your touches in this potential purchase. Imagine getting up in the bedroom, looking out the window, having coffee on the porch. Imagine you in this second home.

There are many major differences between buying a primary and a second home. You probably don't have to worry about school districts, or proximity to work or family, or mass transportation.

Instead, you are asking questions about tax rates, the purity of public water, the availability of lifeguards; seasonal parking, ski patrols; requirements on condo leasing, fishing licenses, dog licenses, boating licenses, dump licenses. (You will be amazed at the license business in small, seasonal, and resort communities.) You also have to check on home water sources and, if you are a fanatic about cooking with gas, the availability of natural gas.

If you are buying in a small town, and if it is historic, beware The Plaque. Your home could have a National Historic Trust designation, or one from the state or even from the town. Whatever the governing body, it is a large red flag. In the National Historic Trust designations, some previous owner has signed over the façade of the house to the trust and received, in return, a tidy little tax break.

That tax break was for them, not you, and that was then, not now. What you get from the trust deal, if you should buy the house, is a mess of restrictions on what you can do to its look. Such a plaque could affect your putting on an addition, changing the windows, adding or subtracting shutters, even changing the front steps from wood to wrought iron. It is a huge consideration. Don't let a seller or Realtor tell you that it's easily handled, that all you have to do is show up in front of a local board or file a few papers. This is sticky business. If you are desperate for this particular plaque-bearing home, take a little time and money and hire a local lawyer. You could do this investigation during the ten-business-day inspection period before escrow opens, something you are going to insist on.

You need that time—especially since nothing is stickier, in thinking about a prospective second home, than what the town will allow you to do with said house. Permits are sometimes close to impossible, particularly in small towns that have experienced a recent remodeling boom. I don't know if it is an attempt to hold on to an earlier feel or look to the town, or simply locals who are really ticked off that the "new people" are coming with truckloads of money and buying everything up. Whatever the motive, many planning boards are resistant and you should check on their policies and any special categories your property is subject to, such as the National Seashore Trust or conservation restrictions or National Park lands or whatever. It is really a matter of "buyer beware."

If all else fails, head over to the town hall yourself. Talk to the people in the tax bureau; try to check with an elected official. Don't make a guesstimate about what will be allowable.

An Afterthought—Selling Your Second Home

You might not want to hear it, but you could eventually sell your second home. Tough commutes, change in family style, a move of your business, or maybe it just wasn't special enough for you.

The reason doesn't matter, but there are some "special" questions you have to answer and some qualms you have to settle before you sell.

- Once you are ready to put the house on the market, break one of the rules of primary home sales and don't strip the house of photographs and personal items. Sure, cut down on the clutter. Make sure the books are not spilling out of the bookcases and that the extra dishes aren't piled on the counter. But for most perspective second home buyers, it is a good thing to understand that you and your family/friends had great times in this particular house, that you relaxed and enjoyed it.

- If you have put in new appliances, leave the manuals on the kitchen counter. If you have painted, leave a list of the colors attached to the manuals. If there are good restaurants nearby or a great pizza delivery or take away Chinese, leave the menus with the appliance pile. Update your emergency list, so that the names and numbers of everyone you use for maintenance is jotted down. You want to show what a well-maintained home you have.

- Are you going to be using the second home at the time you put it on the market? If not, how are you going to keep it fresh and lively in the months it will be closed up except for showings? Does the Realtor have a maid service that will come in a couple times a month, just to open the doors and windows and spray some Febreze around? Do you have a neighbor who would perform the same tasks—or could the agent do it?

■ Before you put the house on the market, make a firm list of what you will leave and what you will take. Replace anything that is special and will not go to the house, but is attached to the house—replace it *before* the house goes on the market. That means an important-to-you special mirror, light fixture, set of curtains. The potential buyer will only want—and whine about and demand—what they actually see in the house. So get rid of treasures before you invite potential buyers in.

■ Are houses moving in your community? The first casualty of a national financial setback is the second home market. No, not in all cases and not in all communities. But you find out if homes/condos are selling, and if they are not, decide whether you can hold on for a few more months to see if there is an upswing.

■ Is there anything you or your Realtor can think of to tart up the house and make for an easier sale? You never got around to planting those flowerboxes or fixing that front step or making sure the bricks on the patio are firmly set in blue stone. All the little touches that show good maintenance are important, but this is not the time to faux-finish the powder room. Some Realtors might want you to rebuild the second floor. Resist!

Recently, for a slew of reasons, I decided that an apartment we had purchased as our retirement home, in Southern California, just didn't suit our purposes. I had spent a year, mostly on the phone with my over-competent contractor Boyce Godsey, putting in wooden floors, granite countertops, marble bathrooms. It was smashing and fit for the neighborhood but not for our in-house needs, i.e. no separate office and guest room, and a kitchen that did not combine looking with cooking.

So I put it on the market with an incredible realtor, named Barbra Tenenbaum, and I went back East. I never saw the apartment again. I took my profit, when she quickly sold it, and used some of it to have the apartment boxed up and moved into storage, or put it into the new condo I bought right before I left town. One year later, when my new apartment was done, I showed up and moved in.

Don't do this unless you have professionals—movers and a Realtor—of the highest caliber. This is not for the Spacey Student Storage and Moving, unless what you are moving is of no value. (Then why go to the bother of packing, storing, and moving?) And certainly, unless you have a truly professional Realtor—not the Loving Hands at Home folks—don't entrust them with this kind of work.

If You Must Construct . . .

Don't go quickly into this quagmire.

First, rent either *Mr. Blandings Builds His Dream House,* a 1948 classic with Cary Grant and Myrna Loy, or *The Egg and I,* a 1947 yuk with Claudette Colbert and Fred MacMurray. What will you learn? That when big city folks head to the country, they have no idea what is waiting for them.

There are secret rules and information known only to the longtime residents. In small towns, expect service people who have deep abiding hatreds of other service people. Carpenters go to Sanibel Island every winter, so they can't work on your A-frame. Plumbers actually work big-time construction in San Francisco, so they are only available in Mariposa on the weekend.

And even in bigger second home cities, Fort Lauderdale or Santa Fe, there is still a different time concept. You can call it "shore time" or "slope time," "vineyard time" or "ranch time." Craftsmen who work in a somewhat vacation-oriented community just don't seem to have the push to rush the job. My sister Jane believes that when you are sitting behind a pickup truck in a seaside community, and the light changes, and the truck doesn't move— well, he's just thinking about crabbing. Or clamming. Or sailing. There is a reason a good craftsman has moved out of a better-paying urban area, and that reason is usually having time to spend on something he/she wants to do more than their job.

If you are involved in a redo, rehab, or any kind of construction, there will be an even greater lack of pressure when you are not on the job site full-time, whining or winning people over.

A fast aside: I never raise my voice to a tradesperson. First, they know a lot more about what they are doing than I do. Second, they are going to be working on my house, so why should I get them mad at me. Third, they really could mess up the job if you get them mad enough that they walk. Where does that leave you? No place good. Besides which, it isn't nice to be a screamer. No one ever moved a job along faster by yelling. (You are allowed to yell at your spouse, family members, and other close friends. Just get it out of your system before you call the contractor.)

One perhaps apocryphal but probably true example: A well-known Hollywood mover-and-shaker, with an alleged nasty temper,

Bob Pollard of Pollard Construction in Alexandria, Virginia, has built dozens of private residences, from chateaus to cabins. He is a repeat performer with many, many clients, and there is no question that his skill and his patience are par excellence. If you are thinking about building your perfect second home, first check out his checklist. Each is crucial.

- Sewage and water. You have to have it. The first thing that the owner has to establish in the jurisdiction is the zoning. Contact your town's building department and consult a civil engineer. In any contract that you sign, the availability of sewage—frequently a septic system—and water supply should be spelled out. It is the hinge that the contract hangs on. Typically, civil engineers will know what the requirements are and will give you advice you can depend on.
- All jurisdictions—towns, counties, villages—work in slightly different ways. All permits require you to get approval from a local authority and the process to get these approvals can be quite expensive. Calculate those expenses when you are deciding if and when to build.
- Talking to real estate people about the possibility of acquiring permits and permissions is *not* recommended. They just don't know.
- It's best to establish things that are important to you *before* you talk to the architect, because when you talk to the architect they are going to tell you what is important to him or to

Continued on next page

(continued from previous page)

her, not to you. When you are asked what you want, you don't want to answer, "I don't know." What you want should not be the barebones requests—like how many bedrooms. The trick is to describe how you want to live in the place, what your lifestyle should be, and how it should be reflected in the structure that is built. Do you want a wide-open space, plenty of rooms for guests, a gourmet kitchen?

■ If you are not talking about a zillion-dollar palace, go with the local architect, who could be really helpful. You have to go on reputation here just like everything else. Talk to people the architect has done work for and go to see the work.

■ As for contractors, the architect most likely will have ideas about the contractors in the area where you want to build. You could also stop by and get to know the people in the bigger supply houses in the area. They all love to talk about their clients—how reliable someone is about finishing the job, paying his subs, etc.

■ One problem in construction concerns the flexibility of either your budget or your vision. In order to meet your budget, you have to be flexible and not insist on a certain kind of stove or faucet or a very specific tile. Establish a price range on everything from cabinets to coat hooks and stay in your range.

- The biggest must is finding a good carpenter. Whoever is doing the work, that contractor has to have a really experienced carpenter, or several if you are lucky. Good carpentry is really the heart and soul of the house.
- Everybody warns against change orders, but a typical person has trouble visualizing from blueprints. As you see the house going up, you are going to locate your switches and your receptacles. You would be surprised how many we move. And that's because an architect wants everything in a house to look at certain way, only wants to see lights that are in a certain pattern. But the pattern that you want might not fit the architect's vision. And you get to decide.
- It is very important to look at the kitchen. God bless architects—they don't cook. They come up with pretty kitchens that don't work. You've got to keep going over the layout and the design to make the kitchen, and the rest of the house, work for you.
- You must be on site—and not just at the beginning and end of the job. One of my customers drilled it into me: "You get what you inspect—not what you expect."

was doing a three-year reconstruction of his manse. His wife eventually wound up taking over the job supervision and the contractor—as it turned out, very personally. As the job neared its end, she bolted with builder. Left behind was a beautifully executed renovation, except that when the owner tried to open his garage door, his dishwasher started; when he turned on his sprinklers, the stereo blasted.

A tiny piece of pipe that isn't correctly screwed in and . . . well, you are flooded. A window that isn't correctly inserted and you are really waterside.

If you are fixing up a second house you have only two choices: One, you do the work when you are *not on* site. Two, you do the work when you are *on* site.

If that seems not much of a choice, look closer.

If the second house is a two-to-four-hour commute, do it in the off-season. Problems: In seasonally warm areas, the winter weather slows you down if you are enlarging or re-enclosing; you will be faced with trudging to the beach during snowstorms or heavy winter rain; half of the people you think you are going to employ are off to Florida.

If it's a longer commute, you can decide you will live on the property while you—your contractor, that is—works on your house. Or you will rent a nearby apartment or motel. Or you will stay with friends. All of these are bad, bad, bad ideas. You cannot live with real remodeling. The water will be turned off. The electricity will be fudged. There will be dust everywhere (contractors never put up those plastic walls they are always reassuring you about) and paint smells.

You can do most jobs from a distance with the help of:

- A reliable contractor. With one, everything is possible; without one, you are in a deep, deep hole.
- An architect (frequently expensive but worth it).

■ A digital camera, if you get it in writing that the contractor will take pictures every week and e-mail them to you.

■ A nearby friend who will stop by once a week and report
progress.

■ A very tight contract that might even include an end date
and a provision that if the work takes longer, you start
getting money back, as in a negative mortgage. (If you
are able to secure such a promise from a contractor in a
seasonal area, please wire me immediately. It is as close
to a first-class miracle as I have ever seen.)

Your biggest insurance is having a guy who has done work in
your neighborhood, who knows the people who give out the construction permits and what hoops to jump through to get them,
and who has reasonable subcontractors.

Construction permits are as esoteric as Sanskrit or the study of
the Loch Ness Monster. Nobody ever knows exactly how a town's
permitting process works or what the actual parameters are for
increasing a footprint, or adding a story or enlarging a septic tank.

If you are in the process of buying a fixer-upper, especially one
near a body of water, you must talk to a town official, a lawyer, a
local you know well, a respected contractor. They can't tell you for
certain how your permitting process will work, but it is a lot better
than sitting in the living room of a prospective second home and
thinking how glorious it will all be when you enclose the porch,
raise the roof, add a deck—and then finding out you can't. Don't
delude yourself. This is the one place you have to have facts.

If you are already in the possession of a second home and getting ready to redo and remodel, you can go ahead and get those permits months before you begin construction. Remember, some municipalities require that a contractor's name be part of the permitting process, so you might have to hire one—and stick with him—to get your job permitted, under way, and eventually completed.

I have always enjoyed construction. I get into the whole jigsaw puzzle aspect of figuring out a house or a space or even a kitchen. But I have come up against some peculiarities in the building trades, time and time again, on both sides of the USA—so many times, in fact, that I am willing to bet that it is a national situation. I call it "The Revenge of the Subcontractor."

Many subcontractors, somewhere along the way, will approach you as if you were their best friend and tell you that the contractor, who you employ and who in turn employs them, is robbing you. No, not always in big cities, but often in seasonal areas or retirement areas or non-urban areas, where there is a great deal of jockeying for the big bucks and the contractors are the king of the hill, an object of envy. After all, they get a markup on everything the sub does, and in the eyes of the sub (even though they hired said sub) they don't do anything for their fee.

Now you are nervous. And you should be a little antsy, but don't fall for the attack on the contractor. Instead, know what markup system your contractor is using and see if it's acceptable to you.

A markup or supervising fee usually gets figured out in one of three ways:

1. You pay the contractor a flat fee and he has the subcontractors bill you directly, while he supervises the work.

2. Much more frequently, the contractor puts an additional fee on everything except for stuff his staff performs, such as framing and carpentry.

3. More infrequently, the contractor puts an additional fee on every speck of work done on the job.

So you pay your money and you take your choice. If your contractor of choice seems to be charging too much, or won't charge you in a manner you want, then you may have to change contractors. (Warning: Remember, if you are already down the line on the permitting process, this change-partners-and-dance strategy might not work!)

What are the other big dangers in contracting?

The guy runs off with the money, doesn't pay the subs, doesn't get the right permits, and/or just doesn't put enough people on the job. I had an old Victorian house in Georgetown in D.C., where a new kitchen took eight months and it was nothing but cabinets. And this was the big city. I was really ticked until I discovered that two well-informed, mucho-intelligent, and well-connected people I knew wound up paying twice for their kitchens; once, for the guy who ran away, and, second, for the guy who finally did the job.

When you interview the contractor, get him to show you stuff he's done. Aha! But that's just the beginning. Get him to show you stuff he's working on or that he is already contracted for in the next year. It is the only way for you to figure out how much time he actually can give you.

And, again, regarding permits: You have to figure out some aspects of the permit process and make sure the contractor is following the law. If there is a slip-up on the job, it won't be his house that has a stop order on it, but yours. You probably don't vote in your second home town, but you pay taxes and that means that the people at town hall are usually able to at least answer some questions. Remember the rule: Any place that is pretty is going to be complicated.

The beach is the worst because of conservation restrictions. That frequently means that you cannot extend the house's footprint (i.e. the exact lines that it currently stands on). So whatever you are building, it will have a first floor exactly as big as the house that stands there now.

There's a good chance, if you are out in the country or along the seashore that you will be in the land of the septic tanks. The presence of a septic means state regulations and, if you are near the seashore or a large body of water, federal regulations. You must have your leeching field a specific number of feet from the high- or low-water mark or the edge of the cliff or the side of the bay or the banks of the lake. Take this into account if you are planning on enlarging the house or adding to the number of "potential occupants." You must, to qualify for permits, have a sufficient and/or upgraded septic system. Septic system requirements are based on the number of bedrooms; permitting officials determine water usage on that basis, because they determine occupancy on that basis. Septic systems thus frequently limit the number of square feet that you are permitted to extend the house, whether you are building upward or outward.

And on the matter of septics, perhaps nothing is more utilitarian or unattractive than the septic tank's "candy cane," the curved piece of pipe that exhausts the fumes from whatever is happening under the ground. A good remedy is the "Mock Rock" from Plow & Hearth (see their catalogue or Web site). It's available in several sizes and colors. It disguises the pipe and gives new meaning to hiding your problems under a rock.

Any construction should involve an evaluation and upgrade of your electricity. You need a licensed electrician and you need to have a box that will hold not just what you presently have in the second house, but what could be coming down the road. You might think you don't need air-conditioning, and maybe you don't. But you want the ability to put it in because one hot summer week could quickly change your mind. Also, upgraded electricity, along with redone bathrooms and kitchens, is a sure selling point if you decide to move on.

What are the most important rules of remodeling?

■ Never say, "While you are doing this, why don't you just go ahead and do that?" This is an invitation for a con-tractor to send his two older children to a fine Ivy League school. If, as the job progresses, you decide that you want to do more than originally planned or scheduled, then have a major sit-down with your contractor and, again, get the estimates for the new work in writing.

■ By any means necessary, avoid "change orders." Once the job is under way, stick with the plans and the prod-ucts. Try to make all your decisions before the job starts and stick to them. Construction is a stop-and-go process: If you are deciding on a different faucet set in your bath-room, you may have decided too late. The holes are there for a 4-inch faucet set—and that's what will fit.

Sticking with the original plans is even more important in a second home reconstruction, where you can't stop by and check progress every couple of days.

■ Get written bids for everything, especially the change orders. (You will too change something somewhere along the way!) It's just another aspect of staying in control. My Cape Cod contracting friend Dennis Mascetta of Bay Builders does not wait to be asked but always offers a written bid for any additional work or a change order. Make every contractor live by Dennis's rules.

■ Be brave and replace the stuff that is old, rotten, nasty, and worn—even though it is charming, was what drew you to the house, and has a "great look" to it. That includes windows that let in the outside, toilets with ancient water tanks hanging above them, unstable porch rails or banisters, sinks with leaky shaky faucets, and my particular aversion, claw-footed bathtubs.

A diversion to my aversion: Yes, I know how attractive and cutesy ancient tubs can be. But a claw-footed tub is an invitation to a trip to the emergency room. They were made for teeny little Victorian people who didn't bathe that regularly anyway. These tubs are almost impossible for an average-size American to clamber in and out of unless you are a sixteen-year-old gymnast. As a home buyer, you were charmed by the tub and now want to spend $1,200 for (again cutesy) a complex faucet-shower thing that has a plethora of pulls and handles and is so British. But just try to use that gadget to take a shower or wash you hair with the water spraying all around the room and you grabbling for a firm

stance in your cutesy claw-footed tub. If you can, envision yourself bathing your own or visiting children in said tub, down on
your hands and knees beside it, struggling to reach in to get the little tyke clean. Tough, huh? If you insist on retaining the claw-footed
monster, then put a decent stall shower in another bathroom and
restrict the tub to long soaks by sure-footed adults.

As you plan your construction, you come to a fork in the
road. On one side, the fine finish work you are looking for in the
living room, with built-ins around the fireplace and cubbies under
the stairs. On the other, the simple bookcases you want in a couple of the bedrooms or in the TV room. Clever you! You figure out
that you don't have to use the same contractor for both jobs.
You'll get the much-recommended but more expensive guy for the
big job, and the local handyman for the pickup work. No, you don't
have to use the same guy for both, but in the long run, you will
wish you had.

You are setting up an inevitable squabble if you bring two "ex-
perts" onto the same field. Both will find the other's work ap-
palling. In small towns, these can be guys who compete for the
same smaller jobs. Certainly if you want to do "handyman" work
at the end of the construction, feel free. But don't put two "contractors" in the same house at the same time. The inevitable back
and forth between them is not worth whatever savings you think
you are accruing. There will be arguments over tools and access
and even spilled coffee.

While you are thinking about breaking up the job into two
parts, how about this division—bring some of your home-town

expertise with you to your second home. That doesn't mean you have to transport the painter, the contractor, the cabinetmaker. No, you can do it all from the living room of your primary house. If you've maintained a good relationship with your primary house contractor and other skilled tradespeople, and since you are always a source for referrals, you will have no problem getting an hour or two of their time and talent.

Here are some specific ways to get your practiced primary home crew involved in your second home:

- Show your primary-home contractor your plans for your second home, or at least your ideas. Let him look them over for any major fault, i.e. you forgot to put a dishwasher in the kitchen. (Yes, that has too happened to me with plans!)

- Get your primary-home painter involved in choosing colors. David Donor, the world's best faux finisher and my Washington painter, is still helping me choose colors even though I now live five hundred miles away. He knows my taste, and he did extraordinary work in several primary homes. A good painter will help you with color choices and also with advice on paint finishes, i.e. do you really want to lacquer the kitchen in your cottage? (Answer: No. Lacquer chips!)

- Have the electrician you've relied on for years go over the plug and lighting plan. Yes, there might be different requirements in a different municipality or a different state, but he could be the one to pick up the fact that you have no outlets on your kitchen island.

■ Use your usual sources for upholstery or upholstery material, get whatever you need for the second house, and
have it all shipped. I have had curtains, pillows, even
slipcovers made in one place and shipped to another.
You know the quality of the work and you probably know
the discount fabric places better in your own home town.

You can, of course, if it is a commutable distance, have your
home-town contractor or painter get hands-on involved in the second home project. You know the pluses because you know the
workers. The minus is equally obvious and enormous: If you need a
permit for the work you are doing at your second home, you probably will get it quicker and easier if you have a local working on the
project. This is especially true in a small town, where members of
the permitting boards are usually folks with some contracting experience, who certainly don't want a nonlocal bigfooting them. Building inspectors become familiar with the contractors in their area
and they trust the work of the good ones. Thus a seasoned local
gets more credit for work done than an imported unknown, whose
work the inspector may be sizing up with a wary eye. Don't forget
the experience-trust factor. Using the local contractor doesn't always mean you will get the best finish work, or even the quickest
finish. But it does usually mean that you will get the job permitted
and that means done eventually. Isn't that the real object?

Contractors will tell you that to get a good job done well
you need either a very, very good set of drawings that are
extremely complete, down to lighting, plug locations, etc., or you

really need a contractor who you trust to pick up where the plans are lacking.

How do you get a contractor that you trust? If I knew that I would write a book called *The Absolutely Fool-Proof Way to Get a Great Contractor* and would embark on a life of redos. Failing that, there are some questions that you want to ask a contractor who is up for your job.

- How long have you been a contractor?
- Are you licensed? Can I get a copy of your license for my insurance company? How much insurance do you carry? Can I get a copy of that policy?
- Are all your subs legal, i.e. are they people with either citizenship or green cards?
- Will you be on the job when one of your subs is working, i.e. will you be in my home when the electrician is putting in the cans in the ceiling or the fans in the attic? Usual answer: "Most of the time." If you are not on site, then you have to insist that the contractor be there more than "Most of the time." One way to ensure this is to have the contractor use your phone to call you from the site at a regular time every day. And if you are leaving a phone in the house while work is being done and you are not on site, call the phone company and have the long-distance capability turned off.
- Who can I talk to in my neighborhood who has used you for the size or type or style of work I am looking for someone to perform? Would you ask them to give me a call or can I call them? Okay, this is the deal maker or

deal breaker. If the contractor can't come up with a name of a local reference, no matter how spiffy the truck or how smooth his manner, move right along to the next contractor.

■ Can we agree on both a starting date and a completion date? This is key in a seasonal home, where everybody wants their job done by the time they return for the season. You've got to get that completion date in writing in a contract that includes the vagaries that plague remodeling and construction. Only when it is in writing can you deal with the maybes: Maybe the contractor runs into problems on another job—that's nobody's fault; maybe he ordered windows or cabinets that just don't arrive and don't arrive and don't arrive; maybe his best carpenter quit and went to another state. And suddenly you are being told that your job will have to take a backseat to the neighbor's up the hill. You have to protect yourself contractwise from someone else taking your place in the construction line.

Buying in a New Planned (and Perhaps Adult) Community

> "Going where no house ever went before."

The first question is, just who is doing the planning?

Obviously, not you, the homebuyer of the condo or town house or manse.

The second question is, just how many more questions do you have to answer before you figure out if this place is right for you.

Here's a bottom-line list:

- Are the rules so rigid that pets, children, plantings, even paint colors are restricted? Are there rules regarding visiting children and what are they?
- Are the roads and utilities (water, gas, sewer, electricity, cable) already in—and are they already included in the prospective property taxes? Is there an upcoming "special assessment"? If they are not already in, will the wires be put underground?
- If there are several floor plans to chose from, can you get smothered in your ranch style by the abutting three-story palaces?
- Will the maintenance of "community facilities," such as party rooms, pools, gyms, or even a guard at the gate, be covered in your annual membership fees? Can these facilities be closed down if a number of the community dwellers think they are no longer needed or beneficial?
- How will officials of your community organization be elected?
- If pets are permitted, is there a size/weight restriction?

(And how much can you get away with? Bob and I, between houses, once stayed in our friend Diane's town house in the suburbs of D.C. Her neighbor, a delightful woman, had a 150-pound pig sharing her town house. She had purchased the pet, believing it to be a miniature, pot-bellied variety, but that was not the case. She finally located it to a pig-rescue sanctuary on a nearby farm.)

All of these questions should be asked if you are considering a move into a condo or a co-op. If you are a person who never participated in team sports, who doesn't like potluck dinners, or who refuses to read the annual holiday letters from your second cousins, you might want to think twice about embracing the community lifestyle that a planned community imposes.

Homes Overseas

If you have one, just don't tell anybody.

Say you are staying in a quaint little hotel on the Left Bank that has to be reserved years in advance. Or at a teeny farm in far Umbria, run by goatherds.

You can't imagine the number of people you know who will be coming your way if you rent or own a home overseas. One way to get away from that problem is to rent a large house and rent it with your friends. Then there are peers for the kids, the teenagers, and you. That way, too, there are no spare rooms for friends that just "drop by."

There are a couple of "musts" you should insist on, especially if you rent a villa in Italy or a farmhouse in Provençe, where you will be paying for every inch of view and every ounce of charm. You must hire a cook. Many European rentals come equipped with a real staff—others do not. You can deal with washing and clean-

Joan and Marco Weiss are now retired, she as a coordinator of large corporate and social events, he as an international lawyer. But they are busy commuting between their apartment in Chicago and an apartment in the 7th arrondissement of Paris. In France, they're real Parisians, taking the Metro and bus to the opera, to go shopping, to museums, and to meet friends at the many great restaurants where they know the inside phone numbers. Joan says, though, that certain "delicacies" have to be brought from home.

There are certain things that are "musts." Going to Paris, I pack a duffel bag with cans of white, water-packed tuna, because I don't like the French brown, oil-packed tuna and it costs like $5 a can. Decaffeinated ice tea, because you can't get that there. Pickle relish for my tuna salad and when we eat *charcoute*. And always, paper napkins from Costco because they are better quality and much cheaper than the French ones. Coming back, I bring truffles and truffle oil, for a pasta salad and eggs the next morning. And, of course, *marron glacés* and boxes of Parisian chocolates wrapped in gold paper and carrying the name of the candy maker—Weiss! It's like we had our own candy store!

ing up the dishes, but don't even think that you can cook a reasonable meal on that little machine that claims to be a stove and yet has no temperature gauges on the knobs. And where are you going to shop, anyway? Are you going to give up touring frescoes for buying fillets? Sure, the local co-ops that are the hallmark of small-town Italian shopping are great, but you don't want to be bagging Barolos when you can be relaxing. Also, in your planning for your stay, you might want to schedule a few trips into a nearby gourmand shrine—but if you are going to be good tourists and look at what the region you are staying in has to offer, you will be tired at the end of the day and you will love coming home to a stranger-cooked meal in your lovely rental.

If you are vacationing for more than a week, you must have enough cars for the household. Tempers get touchy and suddenly different travel agendas are put forth. Some want to sit by the pool; others want to explore the grottoes at nearby churches. Each family unit having its own vehicle—you can mix and match people together if you are headed out for a big group outing— means never having to say you're sorry you came.

If you are serious about buying a home overseas, there are dozens of books in which wonderful writers are trying to recapture, via a bestseller, the tens of thousands of dollars they laid out in relaying a fifteenth-century stone wall or resurfacing a kitchen floor. They will tell you every detail of how wonderfully difficult it is to buy and restore a home overseas, but in such a charming manner that you immediately want to go out, trowel in hand, and do some masonry.

Ellen Shall, the Dean of the Wagner School at New York University and the former deputy mayor of New York, is a person (obviously) talented at climbing over hurdles. But her many years of co-owning a cluster of homes in Tuscany have left her delighted in her domicile but decidedly unhappy with the state of technological advances in the wine country.

In both renting and buying, Ellen warns, phone service is still casual in some areas, cell as well as land lines. So if it is important for you to be in constant contact with the States, be sure to try your various machines before you build a home office.

"We spent a huge amount of money to get a land-line phone three years ago—and we still don't have one. We are still on hold," she explained. One bright light is that international cell phones work, as does Blackberry service. "But for those who try to use a laptop, they discover that every summer involves a different system."

You don't let any of that negative talk discourage you. No way! You are focusing on the wonderful and not the difficult. But be sure the first person you share your vision with is not an architect, builder, or painter, but an attorney. All the hallmarks of property that have been settled for hundreds of years—transfers, permits, liabilities, neighbors, land uses, historical impediments, vendettas, disputed property lines or lines of inheritance—are waiting to fall on your happy head. And, as many Americans now do, if you are buying a property jointly with friends, you probably need both the services of a European lawyer and the advice of an American one, just to keep things straight on both sides of the Pond.

Despite the absence of Kate Hepburn or Bette Davis, a second home is indeed a drama and you get to play any part you

". . . don't ask for the moon. We have the stars."

Bette Davis, *Now, Voyager* (1942)

want. You get to play house in a place that isn't quite real, to indulge fantasies of family and friends and food and fun, and finally, great peace and relaxation. So when you are sitting with dozens of undecided room designs in front of you, when your walls are blotchy with the seventeen shades of aloe–celadon–sea foam green that you are trying out, when you are standing in the middle of a magnificent mess—take a minute. Go outside. Look around.

It is beautiful. You chose it and you were so right. The beach, the vineyard, the farm, the ski slope, the desert, the prairie, the lake—they're all wonderful and just for you. Enjoy every minute of it—then get back inside and get this place up and running.

Index